READ and Reflect

Academic Reading Strategies and Cultural Awareness

Jayme Adelson-Goldstein

with Lori Howard

OXFORD

UNIVERSITY PRESS

OXFORD
UNIVERSITY PRESS

198 Madison Avenue
New York, NY 10016 USA

Great Clarendon Street
Oxford OX2 6DP England

Oxford University Press is a department of the University of Oxford.
It furthers the University's objective of excellence in research, scholarship,
and education by publishing worldwide in

Oxford   New York

Auckland   Cape Town   Dar es Salaam   Hong Kong   Karachi
Kuala Lumpur   Madrid   Melbourne   Mexico City   Nairobi
New Delhi   Shanghai   Taipei   Toronto

With offices in

Argentina   Austria   Brazil   Chile   Czech Republic   France   Greece
Guatemala   Hungary   Italy   Japan   South Korea   Poland   Portugal
Singapore   Switzerland   Thailand   Turkey   Ukraine   Vietnam

OXFORD is a trademark of Oxford University Press

ISBN 0-19-437729-6

Copyright © 2004 Oxford University Press

Library of Congress Cataloging-in-Publication Data

Adelson-Goldstein, Jayme.
   Read and reflect 1 : academic reading strategies and cultural awareness / Jayme
Adelson-Goldstein with Lori Howard.
   p. cm.
   ISBN 0-19-437729-6 (pbk.)
   1. English language—Textbooks for foreign speakers. 2. College readers. I. Title: Read
and reflect one. II. Howard, Lori (Lori B.) III. Title.

PE1128.A24 2005
428.6'4--dc22

2004054758

Executive Publisher ESL: Janet Aitchison
Senior Editor: Pietro Alongi
Associate Editor: Daria Ruzicka
Art Director: Lynn Luchetti
Design Project Manager: Maj-Britt Hagsted
Senior Designer: Claudia Carlson
Designer: Ruby Harn
Senior Art Editor: Jodi Waxman
Production Manager: Shanta Persaud
Production Controller: Eve Wong

Printing (last digit): 10 9 8 7 6 5 4 3 2

Printed in China

Acknowledgements

Illustrations: Barbara Bastian pp. 11, 12, 57; Annie Bissett pp. 4, 18,
32, 46, 60, 74, 88, 102; Paul Hampson pp. 1, 15, 17, 21, 38, 43, 48,
77, 85, 99.

*The publishers would like to thank the following for their permission
to reproduce photographs and cartoons:* Bettmann/CORBIS p. 78
(Ripley); CORBIS p. 82 (Whitman); John Fortune p. 11 (John
Mole); ©2004 Robert Mankoff from Cartoonbank.com p. 29
(cartoon); John and Lisa Merrill/CORBIS p. 81(schoolhouse); The
New Yorker Collection 1991 Charles Barsotti from Cartoonbank.com
p. 108 (cartoon); The New Yorker Collection 2001 David Sipress
from Cartoonbank.com p.66 (cartoon); The New Yorker Collection
1992 Mick Stevens from Cartoonbank.com p. 52 (cartoon); Joseph
Rank/Cartoonstock.com p. 71 (cartoon); James E. Schuck p.38
(Nunziato flower shop); Jodi Waxman/OUP p. 8 (paper bag).

Special thanks: John Mole, Karen Minot (realia backgrounds).

*The publishers would also like to thank the following for their
permission to adapt and reproduce copyright material:*
p. 4. "Managing Social Anxiety and Making New Friends in
College" used by permission of Willamette University Learning
Enhancement Resources; **p. 11.** "Decoding Body Language" used by
permission of John Mole; **pp. 12.** "Handshaking: Grasp the
Meaning" used by permission of Robert E. Brown; **pp. 22.**
"Befriending Wall" used by permission of AHHerlad.com; **pp. 25.**
This article has been adapted and edited by Oxford University Press
as an excerpt of Trust and Privacy Online: Why American Want to
Rewrite the Rules" by the Pew Internet and American Life Project;
pp. 32. Copyright 1998, *The Washington Post.* Reprinted with
permission; **pp. 39.** "When Work is Family" used by permission of
WNYC Radio; **pp. 40.** "Gene Pool, Talent Pool: Hiring is All in the
Family" used by permission of Fast Company; **pp. 53–54.** From
IT'S NOT BUSINESS, IT'S PERSONAL by Ronna Lichtenberg.
Copyright © 2001 Ronna Lichtenberg. Reprinted by permission of
Hyperion; **pp. 63.** "Stress from Health Center A–Z" used by
permission of the National Women's Health Resource Center, Inc.;
pp. 78. Copyright © 2004 Ripley Entertainment Inc.; **pp. 106.**
Information adapted from Space Science Group at Northwestern
State University.

*The Publisher would like to acknowledge the following individuals
for their invaluable input during the development of this series:*
Lynne Barsky, Meg Brooks, Steven Brown, Anitta Gaye Childress,
Carol Curtis, Glória K. Delbim, Betsy Gilliland, Leann Howard,
Robert Irwin, Daryl Kinney, Nick Lambert, Deborah Lazarus,
Elizabeth Neblett, Yara Maria Bannwart Rago, Jean Rose, David
Ross, Jane Selden, Kathy Sherak, Christine Tierney, Anthea Tillyer,
Julie Un, Laura Walsh

Author Acknowledgements
The authors gratefully acknowledge the skill and dedication of the
Oxford editors who worked on *Read and Reflect*: Stephanie Karras—
for her encouragement during the series' infancy; Amy Cooper—for
the WWs (wise ways) that took the series through its adolescence;
and Daria Ruzicka—for the hours of painstaking problem solving
that allowed the series to make its way into the world.

We would also like to thank Pietro Alongi and Janet Aitchison for
their pithy comments and cheerful support throughout the project.
Last, but not least, we would like to express our gratitude to the
design team at OUP—their hard work shows on every page.

Dedication
This book is dedicated to Norma Shapiro: a gift of a human being, a
wonderful writer, and a dear friend—JAG

Introduction

Welcome to *Read and Reflect: Academic Reading Strategies and Cultural Awareness*

This reading series for high-beginning and intermediate students of English as a second or foreign language has four key goals:

- to develop students' awareness and use of reading strategies
- to increase their academic vocabulary, thus preparing them to read academic texts
- to provide a forum for students to learn about and discuss aspects of American culture
- to increase students' enjoyment of the reading process through a wealth of high-interest texts

This book is ideal for young adults planning to pursue a college education; however, it can also be used by students who want to improve their reading skills to attain a personal goal or to advance in the workplace.

Read and Reflect teaches students to read with purpose and comprehension and to interact with the text as they read. In each unit of *Read and Reflect*, students are introduced to a new strategy that supports the target reading skill (for example, looking at the title and source of a text is a strategy for previewing). Exercises throughout the book have students apply these strategies as they read. Activities in both levels help students develop reading fluency. Level 2 also has specific exercises to develop reading speed.

How This Book is Organized

Read and Reflect contains eight thematic units, each tied to a cultural concept, such as social interaction, privacy, and family relationships. To maximize reading opportunities, each unit contains four texts adapted from authentic sources. These texts have different topics, but are connected to the overall cultural theme. Cartoons, questionnaires, charts, and narrative paragraphs provide additional reading practice.

At the beginning of each unit, the cultural theme and reading goals are introduced. Students are asked what they know about the theme and then discuss their prior knowledge, thoughts, and ideas. Pre-reading activities throughout the book provide background information, key vocabulary, and critical reading strategies that enhance students' comprehension of the texts.

All texts are followed by processing activities that require students to demonstrate their understanding, and to use their higher-level thinking skills to analyze and synthesize new information. Because active vocabulary development is an important part of developing reading proficiency, vocabulary exercises occur throughout the units.

A key feature of each unit is the Read and Share activity. Students read one of two related texts in order to share and discuss what they learned. This activity gives students an enhanced purpose for reading while also providing them with an opportunity to apply the reading strategies they have learned.

At the end of each unit, students reflect on what they have read through three expansion activities: an interview, a charting activity, and a writing activity.

Special Features of This Series

- Academic reading strategies
- Academic vocabulary
- Reading skills and vocabulary recycled from unit to unit
- Adapted authentic materials
- Strategies to improve reading speed
- Collaborative learning opportunities
- Critical literacy development

A more detailed description of these features and the unit activities is included in the Teacher's Notes on page 119. The Answer Key begins on page 113.

We hope you find *Read and Reflect* a useful and enjoyable teaching tool. We welcome your comments and ideas. Please write to us care of:
Oxford University Press
English Language Teaching Division
198 Madison Avenue
New York, New York 10016

Jayme Adelson-Goldstein and Lori Howard

Contents

Cultural Concept	Reading Skill	Vocabulary Objective
Social interaction	**Previewing:** Preview key elements of a text such as title, author, headings, illustrations, and captions to determine what you already know about the text.	Identify synonyms.
Personal space	**Predicting:** Using key elements of a text, ask prediction questions about what you will learn from the text.	Distinguish between nouns and verbs in word families. Identify comparatives.
Family roles	**Previewing:** Preview the first sentence of a paragraph to predict what you will learn. Preview comprehension questions to predict the answers and provide a purpose for reading.	Identify synonyms.
Business practices	**Scanning:** Use signals (such as capital letters and numbers) and symbols ($, %, etc.) to help you scan for information in a text.	Use the suffix -able.
Health practices	**Finding Clues in Context:** Look for clues in a text (e.g., synonyms, definitions, examples, or contrasts) to help you understand unknown vocabulary.	Use the prefix un-.
Individualism	**Inferring:** Use prior knowledge to infer information that is not directly stated in the text.	Use context clues to understand unknown vocabulary.
Education	**Identifying the Main Idea:** Discriminate between main ideas and supporting details.	Distinguish between nouns and adjectives in word families; use context clues to understand unknown vocabulary.
Leisure	**Summarizing:** Ask yourself *Who? What? Where? What happened? When? How?* and *Why?* to help you summarize important information.	Use context clues to understand unknown vocabulary.

To the Student

Dear Student,

Welcome to *Read and Reflect*. The purpose of this series is to help you improve your reading in English. You will:

- learn **reading strategies** that will prepare you to read academic or college texts.

- increase your **vocabulary** so that you will better understand what you read.

- discuss **cultural issues** presented in the texts.

Read and Reflect has thirty-two texts on topics such as body language, stress, and the Internet. These texts come from newspapers, magazines, textbooks, websites, biographies, and encyclopedias. To help you improve your reading, each unit of the book asks you to follow three basic steps: **Get Ready to Read, Read,** and **Process What You Read**.

A Word About Reading Strategies

You use reading strategies to help you understand and remember what you read. Some strategies such as previewing and predicting prepare you to read a text. Other strategies, such as scanning and skimming, help you get information from the text without reading every word. Each time you learn a strategy in this book, practice it as often as you can.

Some Suggestions to Help you Read Better

- Decide what you want to find out from the text before you read it.

- Think about what you know about the topic.

- Look at the title, picture and headings to help you guess what you will learn from the text.

- Read silently and try not to move your lips.

- While you read, ask yourself questions such as *Is this true? Do I agree with this? What does this mean to me?*

- Skip over vocabulary words you don't know. (You will be surprised by how much you understand.)

- After you read, check your understanding. Use the questions after the text or your own questions such as *What do I know now? What is my opinion of the author's ideas?*

We wish you a life filled with good books, good health, and good times.

Jayme Adelson-Goldstein and Lori Howard

Unit 1

Reaching Out

In this unit you will:

● read about the importance of social skills in the U.S.
● learn how to preview a text before you read it

HOW DO YOU FEEL ABOUT MEETING NEW PEOPLE?

A. Look at the cartoon. Where are these people? How do they feel? How do you know? Do you ever feel like any of them? When? Discuss your answers with your classmates.

B. Think about these statements. Do you agree or disagree? Discuss your answers with your classmates.

1. Everyone likes to make small talk about the weather or their weekend plans.

2. Talkative people are happier than people who don't talk much.

3. There are more quiet people than talkative people in the U.S.

1

A. Rate how nervous you are in the following situations. Compare responses with your classmates.

| 1 = not nervous at all | 3 = nervous |
| 2 = not very nervous | 4 = very nervous |

Situation	Rating
a. taking a test	
b. asking a question in class	
c. giving an oral report	
d. talking to a teacher	
e. starting a conversation with a stranger	
f. walking into a party	
g. going on a date	
h. answering questions at a job interview	

B. Guess which word or phrase best completes each sentence. Check your guesses after you read the article on page 4.

1. Social situations include ____.

    a. parties   b. being alone   c. studying in the library

2. Most people are ____ when they have to speak in public.

    a. relaxed   b. nervous   c. tired

3. People who have social anxiety don't like to ____.

    a. study   b. go to parties   c. stay home

4. On college campuses, ____ can help students who have social anxiety.

    a. clerks   b. cheerleaders   c. counselors

C. Put a check (✓) next to the words you know. Ask your classmates for the meanings of the words you don't know. Look up the words no one knows in a dictionary.

____ benefit (n.)   ____ challenge (n.)

____ decrease   ____ eliminate

____ embarrass   ____ extremely

____ stressful   ____ technique

> **Previewing** means looking at different parts of a text before you read it. Four elements of a text that are helpful to preview are: the **title**, **author**, **source**, and **headings**. These elements give you important information about what you will read.

Practice Previewing

Preview the elements of the text. Work with a partner to answer the questions below.

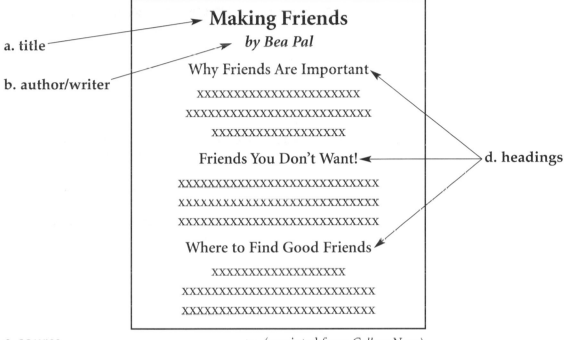

a. title

b. author/writer

Making Friends

by Bea Pal

Why Friends Are Important

xxxxxxxxxxxxxxxxxxxxxxxx
xxxxxxxxxxxxxxxxxxxxxxxxx
xxxxxxxxxxxxxxxxxx

Friends You Don't Want!

xxxxxxxxxxxxxxxxxxxxxxxxxxx
xxxxxxxxxxxxxxxxxxxxxxxxxxx
xxxxxxxxxxxxxxxxxxxxxxxxxxx

Where to Find Good Friends

xxxxxxxxxxxxxxxxxx
xxxxxxxxxxxxxxxxxxxxxxxx
xxxxxxxxxxxxxxxxxxxxxxxx

d. headings

c. source —————→ (reprinted from *College News*)

1. What is the title? What do you know about this subject?

2. Who is the author? Is this a writer you know?

3. What is the source? What do you know about this type of article?

4. What do you already know about the subject of each heading?

Use Your Reading Skills

Take one minute to preview the article on page 4. Then complete these statements. Compare answers with your classmates.

1. From the title, I know that this article is about . . .

2. From the source, I know this article is for . . .

3. From the headings, I know this article has information about . . .

This web page offers advice to students with a common problem.

OUR COLLEGE| *Resource Links*   INDEX   SEARCH   SUPPORT

Managing Social Anxiety and Making New Friends

Resource Links
Academic Advising
Academic Information
Campus Resources
Study Skills/ Tips

Identifying Social Anxiety

Almost all students feel a little uncomfortable or nervous when they have to speak in front of others. It's also common to be a little nervous in a new social situation such as a party or a job interview. Some

5 students, however, become extremely nervous, or scared, before they go to a social event or talk to a new person. They're usually afraid that they won't fit in with the other people or that they'll say or do something to embarrass themselves. In a new social situation, they often wish they could disappear.[1] These students suffer from social anxiety.

10 Fortunately, there are several ways to overcome[2] this problem.

Counselors Can Help

College can be very stressful because there are so many social and academic challenges. That's why students may find it difficult to make friends or take part in campus activities. Counselors at a college's

15 health center can help. These counselors help students practice social skills such as making introductions and making small talk. They also teach students different techniques to fight social anxiety, such as taking deep breaths or relaxing the shoulder and neck muscles.

Four Steps to a Better Social Life

20 Even students without social anxiety may have difficulty making friends. These suggestions can help:
- Introduce yourself to someone sitting near you in class. Ask for his or her opinion of an assignment.
- Focus on[3] the other person during a conversation. Ask about his
25   or her interests and ideas, listen carefully, and give positive feedback.[4]
- Join clubs or groups on campus that interest you. Socially anxious students often find that focusing on a particular activity helps them relax.
- Start a conversation with someone in line at the movies or at the market.

30 Students who practice social skills and relaxation techniques can decrease or eliminate their social anxiety. They can truly enjoy the academic *and* social benefits that college life provides!

Questions or comments? Contact us by <u>clicking here</u>.

Adapted from the Willamette University website.

[1] **disappear:** to go away
[2] **overcome:** to fight against something and win
[3] **focus on:** to give one's complete attention to someone or something
[4] **feedback:** a response to what one sees or hears

PROCESS WHAT YOU READ

A. Choose the phrase that best completes each sentence. Look back at the article to check your answers.

1. Social anxiety can be a problem for college students because they ___.

    a. don't want to make new friends
    b. have many new social and academic challenges
    c. need to see counselors

2. One symptom of social anxiety is ___.

    a. being extremely nervous before meeting people
    b. being a little nervous before a job interview
    c. staying home to study

3. People can fight social anxiety by ___.

    a. staying home and watching television
    b. practicing social skills and relaxation techniques
    c. starting conversations with someone during a movie

4. Another good title for this article would be ___.

    a. "Managing Stress on the Job"
    b. "College Life Is Always Lonely"
    c. "Four Ways to Overcome Social Anxiety"

B. Choose the best suggestion for each problem. More than one answer is possible. Discuss your choices with your classmates.

Your Friend's Problem	Your Advice
___ 1. I never know what to say. I know I'll say something stupid.	a. Introduce yourself to a classmate nearby. Ask a question about the homework.
___ 2. I don't have any friends. Where can I go to make friends?	b. When you feel nervous, take deep breaths and relax your muscles.
___ 3. I don't know anyone in my classes and they don't know me.	c. Focus on the other person and be a good listener. Then you'll know what to say.
___ 4. I get so nervous I can't breathe.	d. Join a club that interests you. You can meet people with similar interests.

5 WORK WITH THE VOCABULARY

A. Choose the word or phrase that has a meaning similar to the underlined word or phrase in the sentence. Look back at the article on page 4 to check your answers.

1. Some students become <u>extremely</u> anxious before a social event.

    a. less
    b. more
    (c.) very

2. They <u>suffer from</u> social anxiety.

    a. dislike
    b. have symptoms of
    c. are free from

3. They often feel that they can't <u>fit in with</u> any social group.

    a. be a part of
    b. focus on
    c. suffer from

4. Sometimes <u>academic challenges</u> can be a problem.

    a. parties
    b. difficult schoolwork
    c. club meetings

5. With help from counselors, students can <u>eliminate</u> their social anxiety.

    a. dislike
    b. find
    c. end

6. Counselors can show these students different <u>techniques</u> to fight social anxiety.

    a. ways
    b. breathing
    c. roads

B. Match each statement to the action it describes.

STATEMENT	ACTION
_d_ **1.** "Your essay is very interesting."	a. experiencing social anxiety
___ **2.** "Sara, this is Paul. Paul, this is Sara."	b. making an introduction
___ **3.** "It's a nice day, isn't it?"	c. asking for an opinion
___ **4.** "What if nobody talks to me in class?"	d. giving feedback
___ **5.** "Do you think this is a good class?"	e. making small talk

6 GET READY TO READ ABOUT: SHYNESS

Take the quiz and compare results with your classmates. Then discuss the questions below.

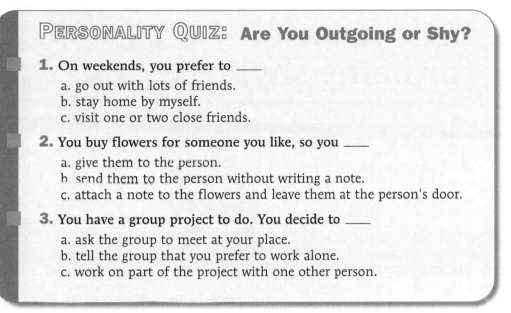

PERSONALITY QUIZ: **Are You Outgoing or Shy?**

1. On weekends, you prefer to ____
   a. go out with lots of friends.
   b. stay home by myself.
   c. visit one or two close friends.

2. You buy flowers for someone you like, so you ____
   a. give them to the person.
   b. send them to the person without writing a note.
   c. attach a note to the flowers and leave them at the person's door.

3. You have a group project to do. You decide to ____
   a. ask the group to meet at your place.
   b. tell the group that you prefer to work alone.
   c. work on part of the project with one other person.

1. Which answers match an outgoing personality: *a, b,* or *c*?

2. Which answers match a shy personality: *a, b,* or *c*?

3. What type of personality matches the *c* answers?

7 BUILDING READING SKILLS: PREVIEWING 2

Some other parts of a text that you can preview are: the **introductory material** above the title, a **photo** or **illustration**, and a **caption** under a photo or illustration.

Use Your Reading Skills

Take one minute to preview the article on page 8. Then complete these statements.

1. The author of this article is ____.
    a. outgoing   b. unhappy   c. shy

2. This article is from a college ____.
    a. website   b. newspaper   c. textbook

3. The title tells you that ____.
    a. too many people are shy   b. it's OK to be shy   c. shy people are unhappy

The following college newspaper article gives one student's opinion about shyness.

Let's hear it for being shy!

Tim Id

THERE'S A LOT OF TALK about shy people right now. Books about shyness are in the bookstores, and there's a lot of discussion about social anxiety on TV and on the radio. I'm a shy guy and I want to say, it's not a big deal. It's just not that important. When I meet new people, I don't talk much; I listen, and I think about what people say. I find out a lot about people that way. While it's true that I almost never start conversations with strangers, I have absolutely no problem talking to my friends. Sure, I blush[1] and my heart beats faster if I have to speak in front of the class, but I'm not alone. I think there are more students like me than students who actually enjoy speaking in public.

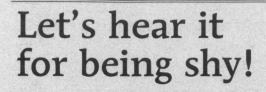

Shy but happy.

What really gets to me[2] is the idea that only talkative people have social skills. You know how often talkative people cut me off[3] when I start to answer their questions? I can't tell you how many times one person in my class will talk and talk and talk, monopolizing the discussion. In my opinion, shy people are better listeners than talkative people. (I heard a talkative guy say that just the other day.)

To tell the truth, at first life on campus was pretty rough. It was difficult because I didn't have any friends and I was lonely. I bought a self-help book.[4] It said shy people should make small talk, so I learned to ask questions like, "Why did you choose this school?" or "What's your favorite class?" I met some great people, and some of them even became good friends, but I never really stopped being shy. It's who I am.

I didn't date much in college at first. It was hard to go up to a girl and start a conversation. Sometimes I worried that I'd say something stupid and embarrass myself or that I wouldn't be able to say anything at all. I thought I'd never find anyone. Lucy became my girlfriend because she came up to me. She started talking and I have never stopped listening.

My idea of a good relationship is one where each person can be totally himself or herself. Lucy agrees with me. We're a good match. She takes me to parties; I take her on quiet walks.

It's going to be a small wedding, and I don't plan on making any big speeches. So, I'm a shy guy . . . so what?

---

[1] **blush:** to have one's face become pink or red (usually with embarrassment)
[2] **get to someone:** to make someone angry about something
[3] **cut someone off:** to interrupt or stop someone from talking
[4] **self-help book:** a book that gives advice on how to deal with personal problems

9 PROCESS WHAT YOU READ

A. Number the sentences in order. Look back at the article to check your answers.

_____ Lucy talked to the author.

_____ The author was too shy to date.

_____ Lucy and the author are getting married.

_____ Lucy and the author go to parties and take quiet walks.

_____ The author learned how to make small talk from a self-help book.

__1__ The author was lonely at college.

B. Write your answers to these questions. Then discuss them with a partner.

1. Is the author male or female? How do you know?

2. Is the author a college student or professor? How do you know?

3. Is the author single or married? How do you know?

10 WORK WITH THE VOCABULARY

A. Review the words and phrases and their definitions. Then use each word or phrase to complete the paragraph below.

a. get to: bother or annoy

b. pretty rough: difficult

c. outgoing: friendly and talkative

d. monopolize the discussion: talk on and on

e. not a big deal: not important

Dear Lucy,

I miss you and your __c__ personality. It's ____ without you. Everyone in class says
                     1   2
hello. Remember that guy Gino? Yesterday he was in my discussion group and he

would not stop talking. He has to ____ every time! Boy, does he ____ me! Well, it's
                                   3   4
OK. It's really ____. I just miss you. Hurry home!
                5
Love,

Your Shy Guy

A. Read this sign for foreign exchange students at a university. Then discuss the questions with your classmates.

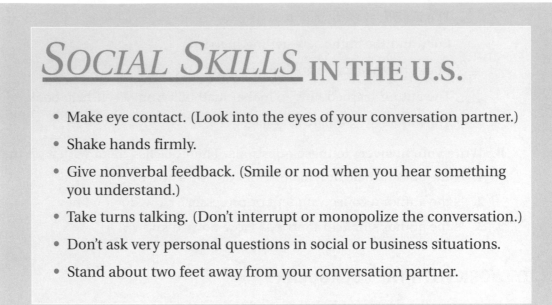

SOCIAL SKILLS IN THE U.S.

- Make eye contact. (Look into the eyes of your conversation partner.)
- Shake hands firmly.
- Give nonverbal feedback. (Smile or nod when you hear something you understand.)
- Take turns talking. (Don't interrupt or monopolize the conversation.)
- Don't ask very personal questions in social or business situations.
- Stand about two feet away from your conversation partner.

1. In your opinion, which three social skills are the most important?
2. Do any of the social skills seem unusual to you?
3. Do you know any different social skills practiced in other cultures?

B. Put a check (✓) next to the words you know. Ask your classmates for the meanings of the words you don't know. Look up the words no one knows in a dictionary.

____ communicate ____ grasp ____ lean

____ nonverbal ____ politician ____ powerful

C. Preview the texts on pages 11 and 12 and answer these questions.

1. What is the connection between the pictures and the topic in text A?
2. What is the connection between the pictures and the topic in text B?

D. Choose one text to read. Then answer these questions.

1. What is the title of the text?
2. What is the topic of the text?
3. What do I already know about this topic?

John Mole is an expert on nonverbal communication. The following information is from his website.

File   Edit   View   Tools   Help

Back   Forward   Stop   Refresh   Home

Actions Speak Louder Than Words

John Mole teaches people all over the world how to understand nonverbal communication. He is an expert on body language; he knows how to read it and how to use it. In his article, "Decoding[1] Body Language," Mole describes how your body language can communicate your interest in what you are hearing or seeing. For example, when you lean forward toward a speaker, you communicate that you want to hear what the speaker is saying. However, when you lean back and cross your arms, you're showing that you're not very interested.

Body language can also show whether a listener agrees or disagrees with the speaker. If you sit with your arms and legs uncrossed, and your hands open, you probably agree with the speaker. On the other hand, crossing your arms and legs and making fists[2] with your hands usually means that you do not agree.

Mole also teaches how to read the nonverbal messages that people send with their eyes, feet, and head. For example, a woman with her head to one side and her eyes half open is communicating, "I'm thinking about what you are saying." A man who is tapping his foot is saying, "I'm getting tired of listening. I have other things to do." A student, slumped in a chair and looking up at the ceiling, is saying, "I'm bored. This doesn't interest me." If someone looks off to the side while he is speaking, you may want to check the information he gives you. This type of body language can mean that the speaker isn't telling the truth!

Mole explains that body language isn't the same in all cultures. There is, however, body language that most North Americans "speak." The pictures on the right may help you "read" people from the United States at parties and at work, but be careful . . . they may try to read you too!

leaning forward

tapping foot

slumping

[1] **decode:** to understand what something means
[2] **fist:** a closed hand

In this book review, the reviewer talks about Robert E. Brown's ideas on different types of handshakes and what they mean.

The Secret of the Successful Handshake

The secret of the successful handshake is no secret anymore. Management Consultant Robert E. Brown explains what shaking hands is all about in his book, *The Art, the Power, the Magic: How to Read Hands That Talk*.

5   For example, to do the *All-American Handshake*, you have to look into another person's eyes, grasp his or her whole hand, and pump[1] it two or three times. According to Brown, this is the handshake of a good listener and trustworthy person.

All-American

10   Politicians and salespeople often use the *Two-Handed Shake* because it's extra-friendly. Two-handed shakers put their left hand on the other person's arm or shoulder as they shake hands. This can feel *too* friendly to some people, so it's best to 15 use it with good friends.

Two-Handed

Watch out for people with handshakes that pull your fingers, or twist and crush your hand. If you get one of these handshakes, the person is trying to intimidate[2] you.

Two more uncomfortable handshakes are the 20 *Palm Pinch* and the *Dead Fish*. A *Palm Pincher* shakes your hand with only a few fingers. In the *Dead Fish* shake, the person's hand slides out of the handshake. It's possible that the people with these handshakes are embarrassed or shy.

Dead Fish

25   Shaking hands is an important part of body language. It can identify someone as truthful, friendly, powerful, or nervous. It's hard to be successful without mastering[3] a good handshake such as the *All-American*. If this isn't your natural handshake, don't worry. Mr. Brown says that you can change your handshake with lots of practice. So, go on out there and 30 start shaking hands. Just think of all the people you can meet!

reviews

---

[1] **pump:** to move something up and down
[2] **intimidate:** to make someone feel afraid and less powerful
[3] **master:** to learn how to do something very well

14 SHARE WHAT YOU LEARNED

A. Work with a partner who read the same text.

1. Read the focus questions for your text.

2. Discuss the questions and write your answers.

Focus Questions for Text A

1. Who is John Mole?

2. What does body language communicate?

3. Give two examples of body positions and what they mean.

4. What are some other nonverbal messages that people can give?

Focus Questions for Text B

1. Who is Robert E. Brown?

2. Describe the All-American handshake.

3. Describe three uncomfortable handshakes.

4. Why is it important to learn how to shake hands well?

B. With your partner, find a pair who read a different text and form a team.

1. Share the topic of your text with your teammates.

2. Take turns sharing your answers to the focus questions.

3. Add any other information from the text that you remember.

15 SHARE WHAT YOU THINK

Discuss these questions with your teammates. Then share your answers with the class.

1. Is body language the same in all cultures? Give some examples of body language.

2. Is it easy or difficult for you to read body language? Why?

3. Do you often shake hands? If so, in what types of situations?

4. Shake hands with your teammates. What kind of handshake did you use?

5. Do you have a story about body language or shaking hands? What happened?

16 REFLECT ON WHAT YOU READ IN THIS UNIT

Interview

Read the questions and think about your answers. Then interview a partner. With your partner, name as many of your classmates as you can.

1. How did you feel on the first day of this class?

2. Did you talk to any of your classmates that day? Why or why not?

3. What else do you remember about that first day?

4. How do you feel in this class now?

Chart

A. Form groups of three. Students A and B: Talk about your plans for the weekend. Student C: Observe students A and B. Use tick marks (⦀) in the chart below to record each time they use body language. After three minutes, change roles.

	lean forward	lean back	look away	look at partner	smile	nod yes
Student A						
Student B						

B. Discuss these questions with the other groups.

• What type(s) of body language did you see most often?

• What other body language did you see?

• How did you feel about someone watching your body language?

• Did you change your body language because someone was watching you?

Write

A. Brainstorm a list of places where it is easy to meet new people. Circle the places you go most often.

B. Write a paragraph that answers some or all of these questions:

• What are some places you go to meet people?

• What do you usually say and do when you meet someone new?

• Do you think it's easy or difficult to make new friends?

• Do you like making new friends? Why or why not?

Unit 2

A Need for Privacy

In this unit you will:

● read about privacy and neighborliness in the U.S.
● learn how to make predictions about a text

WHAT KINDS OF NEIGHBORS DO YOU HAVE?

A. Look at the cartoon. Who are the people in this picture? What are they doing? Why? Discuss your answers with your classmates.

B. Imagine that you're moving to a new neighborhood. Read the descriptions of your new neighbors. Who do you think will be the best neighbor(s)? Explain your choice to your classmates.

1. George is 24, single, and works in an office. When he comes home from work, he plays computer games or watches TV. He keeps his curtains closed and locks his door. He doesn't talk much, except to say "good morning" or "hello."

2. Martha is 42, a single mom, with a 14-year-old daughter. She teaches at a school nearby, and she gets home by 3:30 in the afternoon. Martha often borrows sugar or flour from her neighbors; then she brings them cookies, pies, or cakes.

3. Joe and Karen are an older couple. They welcome visitors at any time of day or night, and they often visit their neighbors to see what is new and to give them advice.

A. Take the quiz to find out how much you value your privacy. Then survey your classmates to compare quiz results.

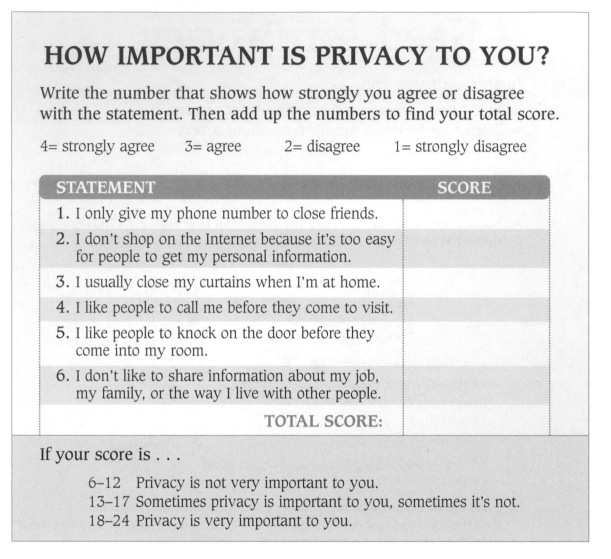

HOW IMPORTANT IS PRIVACY TO YOU?

Write the number that shows how strongly you agree or disagree with the statement. Then add up the numbers to find your total score.

4= strongly agree   3= agree   2= disagree   1= strongly disagree

STATEMENT	SCORE
1. I only give my phone number to close friends.	
2. I don't shop on the Internet because it's too easy for people to get my personal information.	
3. I usually close my curtains when I'm at home.	
4. I like people to call me before they come to visit.	
5. I like people to knock on the door before they come into my room.	
6. I don't like to share information about my job, my family, or the way I live with other people.	
TOTAL SCORE:	

If your score is . . .

6–12   Privacy is not very important to you.
13–17 Sometimes privacy is important to you, sometimes it's not.
18–24 Privacy is very important to you.

B. Read the sentences. Circle the word or phrase that defines or explains the underlined word. Check your answers after you read the essay on page 18.

1. Keiko <u>believes</u> that privacy is important. She (thinks) everyone needs some time away from other people.

2. Alone in her room, Keiko writes her <u>private</u> thoughts in a notebook. She doesn't let anyone read her personal ideas and opinions.

3. When Keiko writes, she expresses herself as an <u>individual</u>, a person who is different from everybody else.

4. Keiko values her <u>right</u>, or freedom, to think and act differently from anyone else.

Predicting means guessing the content of a text before you read it. After you preview a text, ask yourself a prediction question. Use what you know to help you predict what you'll learn in the text. Then, as you read the text, check your predictions.

Preview This	To Predict This
introductory material, title, and illustration or photo	What will I learn in this article?
heading	What will I learn about in this section?

Practice Previewing and Predicting

Look at the text. Preview the introductory material above the title, the title, and the illustration or photo. Work with a partner to predict what you will learn in this article.

Many people who live in the U.S. call before they visit their friends. In this article, the author gives her opinion of this American practice.

VISITING FRIENDS IN THE U.S.A.

XXXXXXXXXXXXXXXXXXXXXXXXXXXXXX
XXXXXXXXXXXXXXXXXXXXXXXXXXXXXX
XXXXXXXXXXXXXXXXXXXXXXXXXXXXX
XXXXXXXXXXXXXXXXXXXXXXXXXXXXXX
XXXXXXXXXXXXXXXXXXXXXXXXXXXXXX
XXXXXXXXXXXXXXXXXXXXXXXXXXXXXX
XXXXXXXXXXXXXXXXXXXXXXXXXXXXXX

Use Your Reading Skills

A. **Preview and make predictions about the essay on page 18. Work with a partner to answer these questions.**

   1. Based on your preview, what is the topic of the essay?

   2. What do you predict you will learn about in this essay?

   3. What do you predict you will learn about in each section of the essay?

B. **Check your predictions as you read the essay.**

This essay explains how Americans feel about privacy, one of the most important cultural values in the U.S.

Privacy, Please!

The Value of Privacy

Americans believe that everyone has the right to act and think as an independent person separate from any group. This is
5 one reason why privacy is very important in the United States.

Some expressions that Americans use show how much they value their privacy. When a person says, "I can do whatever
10 I want in the privacy of my own home," she means that in her personal life, she is free to act the way she chooses. When someone says, "People only know what I want them to know about me," he
15 means that he decides what to tell others about himself and what to keep private. When people say they need time to themselves, they mean they want private time, away from others.

20 ## The Protection of Privacy

Americans protect their privacy in many ways. At home, people put curtains on their windows and fences around their property so that no one can look
25 in. Most people don't want their neighbors to observe[1] the way they choose to live. They like to keep their lifestyle private.

In public places, such as buses or
30 stores, people put up "fences," or physical boundaries. They usually stay at least six inches away from people they don't know, and they don't look into strangers' eyes. There are conversational
35 boundaries, too. For example, some people choose to keep their feelings private, but they talk freely about their jobs. Others share their feelings but don't like to discuss their family problems.

40 ## A Community of Private Individuals

Americans usually see themselves first as individuals, and then as members of a family, community, or other group. These groups are important because they
45 support their members when they need help. However, because of their sense of privacy, and a desire to do things on their own, many people may be too embarrassed to ask for help.

50 Today, communities around the United States are trying to solve this problem. For example, there are many organizations that assist people with language skills, job training, or economic
55 matters. These organizations try to help without asking for a lot of personal information. In some communities police departments teach neighbors how to help each other without being
60 nosy.[2] In these and other ways, people can get the community support they need and keep the independence and privacy they value.

---

[1] **observe:** to watch carefully
[2] **nosy:** too interested in other people's business

A. Choose the correct ending to complete each sentence. Look back at the essay to check your answers.

_d_ **1.** Privacy is . . .

    2. Americans believe they have the right to . . .

    3. At home, people protect their privacy with . . .

    4. In public, people protect their privacy with . . .

    5. Americans usually see themselves . . .

    6. Americans value privacy, but . . .

a. curtains and fences.

b. also need to be part of a community.

c. first as individuals, then as part of a group.

d. very important to Americans.

e. physical and conversational boundaries.

f. act and think independently.

B. Choose the idea under each heading that does not appear in the essay. Look back at the essay to check your answers.

1. The Value of Privacy

    a. Privacy is important to Americans.

    b. Individuals have the right to act and think independently.

    c. Americans rarely talk about themselves.

2. The Protection of Privacy

    a. Americans usually stay six inches apart from strangers.

    b. Americans usually don't talk to people they don't know well.

    c. Different people keep different information private.

3. A Community of Private Individuals

    a. Neighbors can respect each other's privacy and still help each other.

    b. Americans may not ask for help because they value their privacy.

    c. Americans don't see themselves as members of a community.

C. Discuss these questions with a partner.

1. In the U.S., people usually call before they visit a friend or family member. Why do you think they do this?

2. Do you and your friends call before you visit each other?

3. Do you like surprise visits from friends or family members? Why? Why not?

4. Do you think of yourself as a private person?

5. Do you think Americans value privacy more than people from other cultures? Explain.

A. Fill in the missing nouns and verbs in the chart. Look back at the essay on page 18 to find the correct forms.

	Verb	Noun	Paragraph
a.		belief	1
b.		action	1
c.	express		2
d.		protection	3
e.	organize		6
f.	inform		6

B. Choose the correct form of the word for each sentence.

1. a. Americans (believe)/belief) that privacy is very important.

   b. This (believe/belief) affects Americans in their daily lives.

2. a. Americans (act/actions) and think independently.

   b. Their (act/actions) are often based on the way they think.

3. a. The (protect/protection) of privacy is very important in the U.S.

   b. Neighbors use curtains and fences to (protect/protection) their privacy.

4. a. Workers usually (inform/information) their boss when they have to miss work.

   b. They don't usually share personal (inform/information) with the boss.

5. a. The (express/expression) "It's none of your business" means that a person wants to keep something private.

   b. Americans (express/expression) their need for privacy in different ways.

6. a. Many communities (organize/organization) groups that work with the police.

   b. A community (organize/organization) often tries to provide help without invading people's privacy.

C. Match the words and phrases on the left with their definitions. Look back at the essay on page 18 to check your answers.

_c_ 1. boundaries

____ 2. independent

____ 3. lifestyle

____ 4. public places

____ 5. strangers

a. people you don't know

b. where others can observe you (in buses, stores, etc.)

c. physical or conversational "fences" that separate one place or person from another

d. free from the control of anyone else

e. the way you choose to live

6 GET READY TO READ ABOUT: Good Neighbors

Read the conversation between these two neighbors. Then discuss the questions below with your classmates.

> Good fences make good neighbors.

> There is no need for walls between people!

1. Which neighbor do you agree with? Do people need walls? Why or why not?

2. Does a wall make it easier or more difficult to be a good neighbor?

Use Your Reading Skills

A. Preview the introductory material and title on page 22. Then complete these statements.

1. A columnist writes for ___.
   a. radio   b. movies   c. newspapers

2. Columnists often write about their ___.
   a. opinions   b. personal experience   c. both

3. The topic of this article is ___.
   a. farms   b. neighbors   c. writers

4. Befriending means ___.
   a. starting a friendship   b. ending a friendship   c. building

B. Read the first two paragraphs of the article on page 22. What do you think will happen to the author's fence? Discuss your prediction with a partner.

C. Read the rest of the article and check your prediction. As you read, you can also ask yourself these questions.

1. Do I agree with Ms. Barbieri?

2. Would I want her as my neighbor?

Carol Barbieri, a newspaper columnist, wrote the column below to express her strong feelings about fences, walls, neighbors, and neighborliness.

"Befriending" Wall

Carol Barbieri

My husband and I and our two young sons live in a house in a small town. A small town can be a lot friendlier than a big city, but there are "desirable"[1] and "undesirable" neighbors everywhere. I know people who will rush to our house in a split second to help in an emergency. I also live near people who have parties until 5:00 A.M.

Our home used to have a tall fence around it. My mother visited, and she was delighted with the fence. She said, "It's so private. It keeps everyone from knowing your business." (A very strange expression, since my business—writing this column—is open to inspection by anyone who reads this paper.)

Living next door to each other, day by day, our new neighbors grew into our old friends. And guess what? The fences became nothing more than a nuisance![2] Cups of sugar are difficult to pass over a tall fence. So are small children. We realized that we were spending too much time trying to get over it, around it, or through it. What good was it?

"I'm thinking of getting rid of[3] that fence," my husband said to me one day.

"Good idea!" I agreed.

But we had a problem. We needed to keep our small sons safe. What to do?

"Why don't we get a shorter fence?" my husband suggested.

"Great idea," I said.

My parents visited soon after, and they were upset by our new "friendlier" fence.

"Why on earth did you get rid of your old fence?" my mother said. "Are you two crazy?" my astonished[4] father asked. "You took the old fence *down*?" How can I explain it to them? How do I tell them about the pleasant talks, sharing morning cups of coffee, having supper in the backyard with a friend? How do you talk about the laughter at 3:00 A.M., when you and your friend meet each other wearing pajamas? How do you get someone to "feel" the cool summer breeze[5] that you can only experience at that time? Sometimes you just have to look at the moon, because it's so beautiful. Who *cares* if someone is watching? Invite them over to share it with you! A tall fence can take away those opportunities. It's very hard to explain these things to people who love a six-foot fence. Living with friends and neighbors is a joy that happens every day. Good fences *don't make* good neighbors (or good friends!).

Adapted from the *Atlantic Highlands Herald*

[1] **desirable:** wanted, often by many people; worth having
[2] **nuisance:** something that causes trouble
[3] **get rid of something:** to throw away
[4] **astonished:** very surprised
[5] **breeze:** a light wind

8 PROCESS WHAT YOU READ

A. Number the sentences in order. Look back at the article to check your answers.

____ The Barbieris and their neighbors continue to share good times.

____ Carol's parents think the Barbieris are crazy.

____ Carol's mother likes the fence.

____ One reason is that the fence makes it difficult to talk to their neighbors.

____ The Barbieris don't like the fence.

____ They build a shorter fence.

__1__ The Barbieris' house has a tall fence.

B. Discuss these questions with a partner. Look back at the article to check your answers.

1. Why do the Barbieris want a shorter fence? Why do Carol's parents disagree?

2. How does the author enjoy time with her neighbors?

9 WORK WITH THE VOCABULARY

Comparatives: Adjectives

You can use comparative adjectives to compare people or things. For example, *longer* is the comparative form of the adjective *long*. Refer to the chart below.

	REGULAR			IRREGULAR
	One Syllable	**Ending in -y**	**Two or More Syllables**	
Adjective	short	friendly	difficult	good
Comparative	shorter	friendlier	more difficult	better

Underline the comparative adjectives in this paragraph.

Sometimes tall fences are <u>more desirable</u> than short fences. They are more private and make it more difficult for people to see their neighbors. When the Barbieris had a tall fence, it was difficult to be friendly with the neighbors. When the Barbieris put up a shorter fence, they were happier. Carol's parents were upset because they didn't understand that the new fence made it easier to be friendly. A friendlier fence made the Barbieris' life better.

A. **Work with a small group. Think about the differences between a small town and a large city. Complete the chart and then answer the questions below.**

Topic	Small Town	Large City
Population		
Types of entertainment		
Types of businesses		
Privacy		

1. Would you want to live in a small town? Why or why not?

2. Would you want to live in a large city? Why or why not?

3. Is it easier to protect your privacy in a small town or a big city? Explain.

4. Do you think of the Internet as a small town or a big city? Explain.

B. **Put a check (✓) next to the words and phrases you know. Ask your classmates for the meanings of the ones you don't know. Look up the words and phrases no one knows in a dictionary.**

____ accept	____ blame	____ experts
____ false	____ Internet	____ peek
____ personalize	____ reach out	____ similar

C. **Preview the texts on pages 25 and 26 and answer these questions.**

1. What is the topic of text A?

2. What is the topic of text B?

D. **Choose one text to read. Then complete these statements. Check your predictions as you read the text.**

1. The title of my text is . . .

2. In paragraph 1, I predict I will learn about . . .

3. In paragraph 2, I predict I will learn about . . .

4. In paragraph 3, I predict I will learn about . . .

5. In paragraph 4, I predict I will learn about . . .

In a regular neighborhood, fences and walls help people protect their privacy. In the Internet's virtual community, the protection of privacy is much more difficult.

WHO'S PEEKING OVER THE FENCE?

Worries About Privacy Online

Users of the Internet can get information from all over the world. Many Americans are happy to exchange information this way. However, people who value their privacy worry about how easily information moves out of
5 one computer into another. In fact, a study by the PEW Research Center shows that a majority of Internet users (84%) worry about protecting their privacy online. Their biggest worry is that it's too easy for businesses and strangers to access, or get, personal information.

How Cookies Work

10 Actually, it *is* easy for businesses to get personal information. All it takes is a "cookie": an electronic tool that websites use to collect information. When someone clicks onto a website, the site places a cookie on the user's computer. That way a web company can see what users buy and identify their tastes in music, reading, movies, and more. On the positive side,
15 cookies help websites personalize their services. For example, when gardener Joanne Abing clicks onto her favorite online magazine, she sees a list of articles on gardening. Of course, Joanne also wonders why she gets so many e-mail advertisements about gardening. Joanne doesn't know that website owners can sell the information they collect unless they promise they won't.

20 ## Ways to Protect Your Privacy Online

One way to protect privacy is to "tell" the computer not to accept cookies. Users can also give false names or buy special computer programs that keep their identities a secret. Another way is to read a website's privacy agreement before giving any personal information.

25 ## The Internet: A Public Street into Your Private World

Professor Judith Donath, an expert in online behavior, thinks that websites should say if they are private or public. Donath compares this to the difference between being in your own home or walking down the street. For now, though, Internet users should never think they have the same privacy
30 on the Net as they have at home. They need to remember that the private information they put into their computers may quickly become public information for anyone to see.

This excerpt from a textbook compares small town communities of the 1900s with communities forming on the Internet in the 21st century.

Reaching out Through the Computer Screen

■ Life in a Small-Town Community

Imagine you're living in a small town in the United States in 1903. You know all your neighbors by name. Your children go to schools in the neighborhood. When someone is in trouble, everyone reaches out to help.
5 Your family, your friends, your neighbors, the local business people—they're all members of your community. Community is an important part of life.

■ Changes in the 21st Century

Americans had a strong sense of community up until the end of the 20th century; then things started to change. Experts now say that many Americans
10 no longer have a sense of community. It's unusual for people to sit and talk with others; instead they sit and watch television. They usually don't buy from small, local businesses; they shop at big national chains.[1] Most people don't have time to spend with friends and neighbors; they often go to schools outside their neighborhoods, commute[2] over long distances, or spend all
15 their time working at the computer. The experts blame television, business, and technology for this situation. They're right, but they're also wrong. There *is* a sense of community in the U.S., but it's a "virtual community."

■ The Virtual Community

Every day millions of people type messages on their computers in order to
20 make small talk, discuss current events,[3] fall in love, or find new friends. These people form "virtual communities" on the Internet. Each virtual community has people with similar interests, ideas, or questions. One community may focus on a health issue, while another may try to make political changes. Just like neighbors in small towns, virtual community
25 members may start out talking about one topic and end up talking about another. They may also offer help when a community member needs it.

■ Virtual Neighbors

In the 1900s neighbors reached out to each other over fences and across streets. In this century, "virtual neighbors" continue to share a sense of
30 community: celebrating successes, sharing sorrows, or just chatting. They still reach out to each other; only this time they reach through a computer screen, across fences and streets, across cities and states, and across the world.

---

[1] **national chains:** stores located across the U.S. and all owned by the same company
[2] **commute:** to travel regularly between your home and workplace
[3] **current events:** important things that are happening in the world

13 SHARE WHAT YOU LEARNED

A. Work with a partner who read the same text.

    1. Read the focus questions for your text.

    2. Discuss the questions and write your answers.

Focus Questions for Text A

1. Why are some Internet users worried?

2. How do Internet companies collect information?

3. How can Internet users protect their privacy?

4. What do Internet users need to remember when they use the Net?

Focus Questions For Text B

1. Describe life in a small town in the U.S. at the beginning of the twentieth century.

2. Why do experts say that Americans don't have a sense of community?

3. What is a virtual community?

4. Give some examples of how members of a virtual community reach out to each other.

B. With your partner, find a pair who read a different text and form a team.

    1. Share the topic of your text with your teammates.

    2. Take turns sharing your answers to the focus questions.

    3. Add any other information from the text that you remember.

14 SHARE WHAT YOU THINK

Discuss these questions with your teammates. Then share your answers with the class.

1. What are the benefits and disadvantages of being part of a community?

2. Do you use the Internet to reach out to friends and family? Why or why not?

3. Are there any differences between a virtual community and a small-town community? If yes, what are they?

4. Describe the communities you belong to.

Interview

Read the questions and think about your answers. Then work in small groups to interview each other. Decide who has the best neighbor.

1. Think of one of your neighbors. What is his or her name?

2. Describe your neighbor.

3. What do you and your neighbor talk about?

4. Describe a time that your neighbor helped you.

5. What do you like most about having this person for a neighbor?

Chart

A. Look at the examples in the chart. Make a similar chart that shows your roles as an individual and as a group member.

Individual Roles	man, student, artist
Group Member Roles	brother, father, classmate

B. Look at your chart. Which roles are most important to you? Why? Share your answers with your classmates.

Write

A. Choose the topics that you are comfortable discussing in public.

family	hobbies	love	money	politics
religion	school	TV	work	other: _____

B. Write a paragraph that answers some or all of these questions:

- What are some topics you feel comfortable talking about? Why?

- Which topics do you consider personal?

- How do you feel about talking to people you don't know well?

- In your opinion, do people share too much or too little about themselves?

Unit 3

Families That Work

In this unit you will:
- read about changing family roles in the U.S.
- learn more previewing strategies

WHAT DO YOU KNOW ABOUT TWO-INCOME FAMILIES?

A. Look at the cartoon. Who are the people in this picture? What are they doing? Which of them is going to work? Do you find this unusual? Discuss your answers with your classmates.

"You look great. One problem though: I'm the one who goes to work."

B. Guess which number or percent completes each statistic about working couples in the U.S. Check your guesses after you read the articles on pages 32 and 35.

a. 5	b. 10	c. 76%	d. 50%	e. 2,000,000

1. ____ of women worked outside the home in 1970.

2. ____ of women worked outside the home in 1995.

3. ____ men stayed home and took care of their children in 2000.

4. The average husband did ____ hours of housework per week in the 1970s.

5. The average husband does ____ hours of housework per week now.

1 GET READY TO READ ABOUT: Gender Roles

A. Think about these questions and write the answers. Share your responses with your classmates.

1. Look at the list of professions below. Do you think there are jobs that only men can do? If yes, which ones? Do you think there are jobs that only women can do? If yes, which ones?

construction worker	doctor	flight attendant
housekeeper	lawyer	nurse
police officer	salesperson	teacher

2. Which do you think is easier, going to work or raising a child?

3. When you were a child, who went to work in your family? Who took care of the home and children?

4. Do you think men and women are equally good at raising children?

5. Would you want to give up your career to take care of children at home?

B. Guess the meaning of the underlined phrase in each sentence. Match each one with a phrase that has a similar meaning. Check your guesses after you read the article on page 32.

a. equal treatment for men and women

b. divide tasks equally

c. fight for power between men and women

d. an end to

e. an occupation

f. being male or female

__c__ 1. It is possible that the <u>war between the sexes</u> started with the first woman and man.

____ 2. In the 1970s the U.S. government said <u>gender</u> should not stop someone from getting a job, playing sports, or serving in the military.

____ 3. <u>Gender equity</u> helped create more school sports programs for girls and job opportunities for women.

____ 4. Today more and more women in the U.S. are choosing to have <u>a career</u> and a family.

____ 5. Often both partners in a couple <u>share responsibilities</u>.

____ 6. Men and women in the U.S. are working together so well these days that there appears to be <u>a cease-fire in</u> the war between the sexes.

2 BUILDING READING SKILLS: More Previewing Strategies

Reading the first sentence of each paragraph is another way to preview a text. By reading just those first sentences, you can learn a lot about the whole text. This is a helpful strategy when there are no headings or illustrations to preview.

Practice Previewing and Predicting

A. Read the passage below. It is the first sentence of paragraph 1 in the article on page 32.

A Cease-Fire in the War Between the Sexes

Thanks to the 20th-century battles[1] for gender equity, there are more women in the workplace and more men taking care of children and the home.

B. Circle three facts that you learned from the sentence above.

a. Gender equity was an important topic in the 20th century.

b. There are now more women in the workplace.

c. Women are fighting with men.

d. More men are taking care of children and the home.

e. There were many wars in the 20th century.

C. Form groups of five. Assign one paragraph from page 32 to each person. Preview the first sentence of your paragraph and share that information with your group.

Use what you learned from your preview to make predictions. Put a check (✓) next to the ideas you predict will be in the article.

____ **a.** Gender equity is increasing.

____ **b.** Men are doing less housework.

____ **c.** Younger people believe in gender equity.

____ **d.** It's easy to work and have a family.

____ **e.** Life was better in the past.

USE YOUR READING SKILLS

A. Read the article and check your predictions above as you read.

B. As you read the article, underline any information that shows your predictions were right.

This newspaper article discusses a recent survey on gender roles. It's based on a series of Washington Post *stories by Richard Morin and Megan Rosenfeld.*

A Cease-Fire in the War Between the Sexes

Thanks to the 20th-century battles[1] for gender equity, there are more women in the workplace and more men taking care of children and the home. The results of a national survey[2] by Harvard University show that gender equity is increasing. It also shows that modern life in the United States creates stress
5 for both sexes. Interestingly, 66% of the survey respondents said that couples need two incomes.

With more and more women joining the workplace, men's traditional roles are changing. These days, American men are doing more around the house than their fathers ever did. In the 1970s the average husband did five hours of
10 housework a week. That number is now up to ten hours. The survey showed, however, that these changes do not create gender equity. Couples with children say that the women still do most of the shopping, laundry, cooking, cleaning, errands,[3] and caring for children—even when both parents work full-time.

Age more than gender determines how a person feels about the changing
15 **gender roles.** The survey found that, in general, Americans born after 1960 have a more positive attitude toward gender equity. They believe that it makes their lives better. They also believe that a woman's life should include a job or career.

Changing roles means sharing responsibilities such as cooking, caring for children, shopping, and paying bills. Some people, like warehouse worker John
20 Lindow, worry that all these responsibilities can make married life hard. "By the time you get done with your job, you have to rush home and make supper, do whatever, and then you have to drive your kids somewhere else. You don't get enough time to spend with your wife anymore. . . . You're lucky if you get to see her one or two hours a day. What kind of quality time is that?"

25 **Changing gender roles may bring stress, but a majority of respondents said they didn't want to return to the past.** They didn't want to go back to a time with fewer workplace opportunities for women. As Jennifer Weberg, 25, a graphics designer, put it: "It would be a shame if things went back to the way they were in the fifties. . . . It's easier to grow up knowing that some day you're
30 just going to get married and be a mom or a wife, and now it's more complex. You have to figure out what you want to do with your life. . . . But I think having more choices is always a good thing."

[1] **battle:** a fight between two people or groups
[2] **survey:** a set of questions about peoples' opinions and behavior
[3] **errand:** a short trip to do a simple task, such as mailing a letter

4 PROCESS WHAT YOU READ

A. Each sentence below is incorrect. Cross out the word that makes the sentence incorrect and replace it with the correct word. Look back at the article to check your answers.

1. Compared to the 1950s, there are more ~~men~~ *women* in the workplace now.

2. These days American men are doing less housework than their fathers ever did.

3. Attitudes about the changing roles of men and women are based mostly on gender.

4. Most people born after 1960 think men's and women's new roles make life worse.

5. Some people worry that the new responsibilities make marriage easier.

6. Most people want to go back to a time with fewer workplace opportunities for women.

B. Reread paragraphs 2, 3, and 4 in the article and choose a heading for each one. Share your answers with the class. Discuss why some headings are better than others.

Paragraph 2

    a. Couples Get New Roles   b. Everything Changes   c. From Five to Ten

Paragraph 3

    a. Age = Attitude   b. Changes Make Lives Better   c. The 1960s

Paragraph 4

    a. Better but Not Easier   b. Changes Bring Worries   c. A Sweet Life

C. Discuss these questions with a partner.

1. What information did you learn from the article?

2. Was the information new or interesting to you?

3. How do you think the authors feel about gender equity? Why?

5 WORK WITH THE VOCABULARY

Cross out the word that does not belong in each word set.

1. ~~age~~   male   gender   female
2. battle   agreement   fight   war
3. couple   pair   two   single
4. income   money   fines   salary
5. career   job   profession   workplace

6 GET READY TO READ ABOUT: Stay-at-Home Dads

Guess which word completes each sentence. Check your guesses after you read the article on page 35.

a. percentage	b. rewarding	c. jealous	d. provider

1. She hates it when her boyfriend smiles at other women. She's ____.

2. In a group of 100 happily married couples, the ____ of people who said they talk about their problems was high—88 percent.

3. Some couples take turns being the family's ____. One year the husband goes out to work, the next year the wife works.

4. Being a parent can be very ____. It's wonderful to watch a child develop into an adult.

7 BUILDING READING SKILLS: Previewing Questions

> **Comprehension questions** often follow a text to help you check how well you understood the material. You can also preview the questions *before* you read the text. Then as you read, you can look for the answers and use a highlighter to mark them in the text.

Practice Previewing Comprehension Questions

Read the comprehension question before you read the text below. Then read the text and highlight the answer.

In the U.S., approximately how many fathers stay at home to take care of their children?

    a. 200   b. 2,000,000   c. 2   d. 2,000

> *In some families one partner works outside the home (usually the one with the better-paying job), while the other partner takes care of the kids. Sometimes the stay-at-home partner is the dad. In 2002 there were more than 2 million stay-at-home dads.*

Use Your Reading Skills

1. **Preview the article on page 35 and the questions on page 36.**

2. **As you read the article, highlight the answers.**

This book review talks about a book by a stay-at-home dad.

BOOK REVIEW

BOOK REVIEW

Mark Wertman's
True Confessions of a Real Mr. Mom

Who Works? Who Stays Home?

Most Americans agree that the workplace and the home are very different from the way they were thirty years ago. The world of work is no longer a man's world. Between 1970 and 1995, the percentage of women who worked outside the home went from 50 percent to 76 percent.[1] In the year
5 2000, of the more than 55 million married couples in the United States, 10.5 million women were making more money than their husbands, and 2 million men were stay-at-home dads.[2]

Author, husband, and father Mark Wertman writes about being a stay-at-home dad in his book *True Confessions of a Real Mr. Mom.* His
10 story will help others who are learning how to live with the changing gender roles in our society.

Mark and his wife, Georgine, were a two-income couple, but things changed when their first baby was born. Georgine wanted to continue her work as a lawyer, but someone needed to stay home to take care of the baby.
15 Georgine had the higher paying job, so she became the provider. Mark stayed home to raise the children. In his book he tells many stories about his role in the family.

At first, it was difficult to change roles. The Wertman kids often went to Mark first to talk about their problems. Georgine was jealous of the time
20 the children spent with their father. Mark had some hard times too. People often asked him, "When are you going to get a real job?" Even in the 21st century, society respects the role of provider more than the role of child raiser. Mark found out all about this.

Mark and Georgine learned that it is very important to talk about
25 **their problems.** In the beginning, Mark thought Georgine had the easy job, and Georgine thought that Mark had it easy. Later they talked it over and discovered that both jobs were difficult and rewarding. Georgine and Mark agree that talking things over and making decisions together helps their relationship.

The Wertmans are happy with the results[3] of their decision.
30 Their children are ready for a world where men and women can choose their roles. Wertman's book is entertaining and educational, especially for couples who want to switch roles. As Mark Wertman says "*We* are society. *We* make the changes one by one. People have to decide on what's best for them and their families." ▫

[1] This statistic is for women ages 24–54 (from Bianchi and Spain, *Balancing Act*, 1998).
[2] This research is quoted in the October 2001 issue of *American Psychologist*.
[3] **result:** something that happens because of something else

A. Choose the correct answer to each question. Look back at the article on page 35 to check your answers.

1. Why is the workplace no longer a man's world?
   a. More women are jealous.
   b. Men are not strong.
   c. Fewer men are stay-at-home dads.
   d. More women are in the workplace.

2. What is Mark Wertman's book about?
   a. his writing job
   b. his life as a stay-at-home dad
   c. his first baby
   d. his wife's job

3. Why is Georgine the provider in the family?
   a. Mark does not want to be the provider.
   b. Mark lost his job when their first baby was born.
   c. She had the higher paying job when their first baby was born.
   d. None of the above.

4. Why was it difficult for the Wertmans to change roles?
   a. They were jealous of each other's jobs.
   b. The children went to their dad for help first.
   c. People respect the provider.
   d. All of the above.

5. How do the Wertmans work out their problems?
   a. They make their jobs easier.
   b. They talk and make decisions together.
   c. They change jobs.
   d. They help their children.

6. How do the Wertmans feel about their decision?
   a. They're happy because they're entertaining.
   b. They're happy because their children are ready for the modern world.
   c. They're unhappy because they want to change jobs.
   d. They're unhappy because people don't respect Mark.

B. Discuss your answers to these questions with your classmates.

1. Would you be happy with the Wertmans' lifestyle? Why or why not?

2. Does the reviewer like Mark Wertman's book?

Read the diary entries of stay-at-home dad Gary Sanders, and complete the statements with the correct words.

> Tuesday, 10 P.M. Today was the same as yesterday. Jill went off to work. I got Emily up and off to school, shopped, cooked, cleaned, did the laundry, ran errands, picked up Emily at 3:00 and took her to her piano lesson. When I got home at 5:00, I made dinner and helped Emily with her homework. Jill worked late, so I fixed her a snack around 9:00. It's 10:00 and I'm ready for bed!

1. Jill goes off to work because she is the ____.
   a. provider   b. wife   c. homemaker   d. stay-at-home mom

2. Gary is tired because of his ____.
   a. daughter   b. gender   c. decisions   d. responsibilities

> Wednesday, 11:30 P.M. It was a late night and a hard one. Emily had a big project for school and I helped her research information on the Internet. Jill wanted to help too, but Emily said that one parent's help was enough. Jill was unhappy and started arguing with Emily. I told them to stop fighting. We usually talk things over, but sometimes the change in roles is hard on all of us.

3. When Emily told Jill that she only wanted her dad's help, Jill was probably ____.
   a. worried   b. jealous   c. exhausted   d. happy

4. When Jill and Emily were fighting, Gary called for ____.
   a. a doctor   b. a war   c. help   d. a cease-fire

> Friday, 11:00 P.M. What a week! Emily got an A+ on her project. Jill got a promotion at work. We celebrated with pizza and my special chocolate chip cookies. Emily and Jill did the dishes after dinner. Then, Emily played piano, and Jill and I sat and talked. I have the best job in the world, but I'm glad the weekend is here!

5. Right now, Gary's career is being a ____.
   a. cook   b. teacher   c. driver   d. stay-at-home dad

6. When Gary's family is happy, he finds his job ____.
   a. tiring   b. responsible   c. rewarding   d. difficult

A. The people in each picture work together. Guess where they work and how they are related. Share your ideas with your classmates.

B. Put a check (✓) next to the words you know. Ask your classmates for the meanings of the words you don't know. Look up the words no one knows in a dictionary.

Family Vocabulary

___ cousin

___ generation

___ nephew

___ related

___ siblings

Business Vocabulary

___ corporate director

___ employee

___ fail

___ supervise

___ unsuccessful

C. Preview the texts on pages 39 and 40 and answer these questions.

1. What is the topic of text A?

2. What is the topic of text B?

D. Choose one text to read. Preview the focus questions for your text on page 41. Predict the answer to the first question. Then, highlight the answers to each question as you read the text.

I will probably find the answer to . . .

1. question 1 in paragraph(s) ___

2. question 2 in paragraph(s) ___

3. question 3 in paragraph(s) ___

4. question 4 in paragraph(s) ___

About 90 percent of all businesses in the U.S. are run by families. For these families, work isn't something that separates them; it's what keeps them together.

WORK: The glue that keeps a family together

Michael and Neil Gioia are brothers, but they are also business partners. They are the third generation to run the family business, Nunziato Florists,[1] in Woodside, New York. The Gioias' grandparents started the small shop in 1913. The business keeps this Italian-American family laughing and working together.

5 **R**unning a family business is hard work. Michael and Neil work long days every day. Their mother, Nikki, is in her eighties and works right beside them. The Gioias live near the shop. There are no days off, no family vacations. They work hard, they work together, and their business succeeds.

Not all family businesses do so well. In fact, only three out of ten family
10 businesses make it.[2] There are often problems. Sometimes siblings fight over the business, and sometimes the family just doesn't have a good business plan.[3] Many family businesses fail because the younger generation just isn't interested.

The Gioias lives are all about their family business. In an interview with Carlos Briceno, of radio station WNYC, Neil Gioia explains why he lives two
15 blocks away from the shop. "Since it's a seven-day-a-week business, you have to work ten to twelve hours a day. If I lived any farther away, it would be impossible for me to get home to have any kind of family life."

Michael, Neil's younger brother, is in his 40s, but he still remembers making Christmas wreaths[4] for the shop when he was seven. He believes
20 that working in a family business is good for a child. "When you get older and look back at it, and you see the type of person you are now, why is that? Why are you that way? It's because of the way you were raised, with your family around." Michael says he had time to play as a child, but he also enjoyed being with his family and helping out at the store. Michael believes the shop taught him responsibility.

25 **T**he Gioia brothers have a young nephew, Mikey, who likes being in the shop with his uncles and other relatives. He started working when he was five. He arranges flowers for his teachers and sweeps the floor. The Gioias know that in any family business, the key to success is the next generation. For the Gioias, little Mikey may be that key.

[1] **florist:** a flower shop
[2] **make it:** to succeed
[3] **business plan:** a plan for the future of a business
[4] **Christmas wreath:** a circle of leaves and flowers, often put on doors at Christmastime

Most companies use the term "corporate family" to describe the team spirit of their employees. However, when some companies say "corporate family" they mean it! This magazine article explains why some companies think having employees from the same family is a good idea.

Hiring
Is All in **the Family**

"We believe in nepotism"[1] says Sherry Phelps, Southwest Airline's director of corporate employment. "We encourage people to recommend family members who might make good employees. Our only rule is that one family member can't supervise another."

5 For some employers, the idea of hiring family members sounds like trouble. They worry about fights between couples, battles between siblings, or favoritism.[2] Southwest Airlines doesn't see it that way. They believe the best new employees will be the relatives of their best employees.

There are three basic reasons why some companies hire family members:

10 The Talent is in the Genes.[3]

Ann Rhoades, of the DoubleTree Hotel company says, "If you have a mother who is a great worker, chances are her daughter is going to be a great worker." She means that people in the same family often have the same good qualities.

15 It's Difficult to Lie to Your Mother.

Family ties keep employees honest. Family members usually don't sugarcoat[4] the truth. Phelps gives this example: A Southwest employee called her and said, "I want to tell you about my son. Do not hire him. He's lazy. He won't make a good Southwest employee."

20 Families That Work Together Stay Together on the Job.

It's hard to keep good people. However, when family members are happy at the same organization, they're less likely[5] to leave. Another business that hires family is Quad/Graphics. This company employs hundreds of married couples, brothers, sisters, sons, daughters, and cousins. In fact, more than 50% of the 25 employees are related to each other! The company also has over $2 billion in sales, 14,000 employees, and 22 facilities on three continents.

With these kinds of statistics, it's easy to understand why some companies think of themselves as "one big happy (and successful) family."

---

[1] **nepotism:** the practice of a person in power who gives family members good jobs in his or her company
[2] **favoritism:** special treatment for friends or family
[3] **gene:** the cell that passes on hair color, eye color, personality, etc., from parent to child
[4] **sugarcoat:** to make something sound better or sweeter than it is
[5] **less likely:** probably not going to happen

14 SHARE WHAT YOU LEARNED

A. Work with a partner who read the same text.

    1. Read the focus questions for your text.

    2. Discuss the questions and write your answers.

Focus Questions for Text A

1. Give three reasons why most family businesses fail.

2. What type of business does the Gioia family own? Who runs the business?

3. Why is the Gioia family business successful?

4. Why do Neil and Michael Gioia think that working in a family business is good for children?

Focus Questions for Text B

1. What problems can occur when family members work together?

2. Which three companies does the article name?

3. Give three reasons why some companies like to hire members of the same family.

4. How do companies know that hiring families is good for business?

B. With your partner, find a pair who read a different text and form a team.

    1. Share the topic of your text with your teammates.

    2. Take turns sharing your answers to the focus questions.

    3. Add any other information from the text that you remember.

15 SHARE WHAT YOU THINK

Discuss these questions with your teammates. Then share your answers with the class.

1. Does your family own a business? If yes, what kind of business is it? If not, did you ever think about having a family business? What kind?

2. Do you think it's a good idea for young children to work with their families? Why or why not?

3. What kind of businesses are good for families to run? Why?

4. What are the benefits of working in a business where no one is related?

Interview

Read the questions and think about your answers. Then interview a partner. With your partner, discuss which is easier, going to work or raising a child.

1. When you were a child, who went to work in your family? Who took care of the children?

2. Did you work when you were a child? If yes, what kind of work did you do?

3. Do you know any couples with children? If yes, which of the parents work?

Chart

A. Work in small groups. Think of positive, negative, and interesting aspects of families working together. Look at the statements in the chart. Write two more ideas in each section of the chart.

FAMILIES WORKING TOGETHER		
Positive	**Negative**	**Interesting**
Children learn responsibility.	Children have to go to school and work in the business.	Children find out if they like their parents' business.

B. Share your ideas with your classmates.

Write

A. Work with a small group to discuss the following questions.

- In the past, which jobs were "men's work" and which jobs were "women's work"?

- Do you see a difference in job opportunities for men and women now? Explain.

B. Write a paragraph that answers some or all of these questions:

- Do men and women have different abilities? If yes, what are they?

- What examples of gender equity do you see in your daily life?

- In general, is gender equity a good idea? Why or why not?

Unit 4

Staying in Business

In this unit you will:

- read about business in the U.S.
- learn how to scan a text for specific information

WHAT DO YOU KNOW ABOUT BUSINESS?

A. Talk about the picture with a partner. What kind of business do you think this is? What are the employees doing? Which person is the boss? How do you know?

B. Think about these questions. Discuss your answers with your classmates.

1. Name as many major U.S. companies as you can.

2. What are the most popular items to buy right now? Which companies produce them?

3. Imagine you can own any business you like. Which business would you choose?

1 GET READY TO READ ABOUT: Business in the U.S.

A. Guess which statements are true. Check your guesses after you read the article on page 46.

Statement	True	False
1. Small business in the U.S. started in 1860.		
2. In the 1860s, new machines started to produce items quickly and cheaply.		
3. The national railroad hurt U.S. business.		
4. Immigration helped business grow in the U.S.		
5. In the early 1900s workers in the U.S. made a lot of money.		
6. There were no millionaires in the U.S. before the 1860s.		
7. The U.S. government has hundreds of rules that businesses must follow.		
8. U.S. businesses are not interested in safety.		

B. Guess the meanings of the underlined words or phrases in the sentences. Check your answers after you read the article on page 46.

1. <u>Consumers</u> usually want to buy computers that have all the latest features for a low price.

    a. customers   b. salespeople

2. Nowadays almost everyone buys a computer, so some computer businesses <u>have huge profits</u>.

    a. lose a lot of money   b. make a lot of money

3. Businesses that make computers have to follow government <u>regulations</u>.

    a. occupations   b. rules or laws

4. There are many different computer <u>products</u> for the home office, including scanners, printers, and modems.

    a. items for sale   b. stores

5. In today's fast-changing technology, someone <u>invents</u> something new for the computer every day.

    a. creates a new item   b. fixes something

6. The average <u>wage</u> for a computer repair person is $35.00 per hour.

    a. price   b. pay

> **Scanning** means looking for specific information in a text. When you scan, you move your eyes quickly down the page to look for specific words or signals that will lead to the information you want. The signals can be capital letters (for names and places), numbers (for dates, times, prices, etc.) or symbols ($, %, etc.).

Practice Your Scanning Skills

A. Scan the ad for capital letters to answer these questions.

1. What is the name of the musical light bulb? _____

2. Who is the inventor of the musical light bulb? _____

B. Scan the ad for numbers to answer these questions.

1. How many songs does each light bulb play? _____

2. How many bulbs are in a gift pack? _____

C. Scan the ad for $ and % symbols to answer these questions.

1. How much does a musical light bulb cost? _____

2. How much of a refund can you get if you're not satisfied? _____

MUSICAL LIGHT BULBS ARE HERE!

Melodylights are the musical light bulbs invented by opera singer, Domino Parroti. Melodylights play music whenever you switch them on. There are 12 different songs on each bulb! Melodylights cost $2.95 plus shipping and handling. Gift packs of 10 are available. To order, call us today at 800-505-5555 or go to our website, www.melodylight.com. We offer a 100% refund if you're not satisfied! Turn on the light *and* the music with Melodylight!

Use Your Reading Skills

A. Preview the article on page 46. What is the topic of the article?

B. Scan the article for the answers to these questions.

1. How many immigrants came to the U.S. between 1870 and 1916? _____

2. How many millionaires were there in the U.S. in 1850? _____

The growth of Big Business is an important part of American history. This encyclopedia entry explains why.

U.S. Business History—
From Small Business to Big Business

In the 1860s American business started to change. Before that time most businesses were small; they made products by hand and sold them to local[1] customers. Beginning in the 1860s, inventors created new machines that could produce clothing, canned foods, tools, and other items quickly and cheaply. By
5   making large quantities of items in less time, companies could spend less money on production. This made it possible to charge lower prices. In addition, a new national railroad allowed businesses to sell their products to people all across the country. The combination of fast production, low production costs, inexpensive products, and a whole nation of consumers helped small businesses
10   grow into big businesses. This time in history was called The Age of Big Business.

Big Business continued to grow because of three things: more products, more customers, and more money. The typewriter, the light bulb, and the telephone were important inventions that became very popular products. Thanks to the 25 million immigrants that came to the United States between
15   1870 and 1916, there were many new customers to buy these products. Businesses made huge profits from the sales of their products to large numbers of people. They used these profits to build more factories, which in turn, produced more items to sell.

The owners of these businesses became very rich. In 1850 there were 20
20   millionaires in the United States; by 1900 there were more than 3,000. However, the workers who made the new products were very poor. They had little money for housing, food, clothing, and medical care. These workers usually worked at least 60 hours a week for an average pay of about 20 cents an hour. Not only were their wages low, but their workplaces were very dangerous.

25   In the early 1900s reformers[2] helped workers organize labor unions[3] to improve working conditions and wages. Reformers also asked the government to protect both workers and consumers with safety regulations. They wanted every business to guarantee[4] the safety of its workplace and its products. The reformers were successful—by the 1960s, there were hundreds of government
30   regulations that businesses had to follow.

---

[1] **local:** nearby, in the area of the business
[2] **reformer:** a person who wants to make bad conditions in society better
[3] **labor union:** a group that represents the needs of all the workers in that group
[4] **guarantee:** to promise that something is true or will happen.

The reforms and regulations of the 20th century continue to affect American business. Business owners still look to inventions and new technology to help them make more money, but the importance of safety means that companies have to think about profits *and* people. It's this kind of thinking that helps
35 America stay in business.

4 PROCESS WHAT YOU READ

A. Choose the correct answer to each question. Look back at the text to check your answers.

1. When did Big Business start?

    a. before 1860　　　　　　b. in the 1860s　　　　　　c. both

2. Why did the number of consumers increase between 1870 and 1916?

    a. immigration increased　　b. there were more millionaires　　c. both

3. What did reformers want to change?

    a. workers' conditions　　　b. workers' pay　　　　　　c. both

4. What do U.S. businesses still look for today?

    a. ways to use technology　　b. places to sell their products　　c. both

B. Work with a partner to answer the questions. First, answer based on what you remember. Then, scan the text to complete or check your answers.

1. Name three things that helped Big Business grow.

2. How many millionaires were there in 1900?

3. What was the average worker's pay during the Age of Big Business?

4. How many hours long was the average workweek at that time?

5 WORK WITH THE VOCABULARY

Cross out the word that does not belong in each word set.

1. improve	promise	guarantee
2. buyer	owner	consumer
3. sell	produce (*v.*)	make
4. profit	rule	regulation
5. pay	conditions	wages
6. work	invent	create

GET READY TO READ ABOUT: A Business

A. Match the words to the things or actions in the picture.

1. blow (one's) nose _a_   2. handkerchief ___   3. makeup ___

4. remove ___   5. tissue ___

B. Work with a partner to brainstorm different ways to use tissues. Present one idea from your list to the class and say why it is a good idea.

Use Your Reading Skills

A. Preview the article on page 49 to complete these statements.

1. This article is about the history of ___.

 a. the telephone   b. Kleenex tissues   c. World War I

2. Kimberly-Clark is a ___.

 a. company   b. woman   c. magazine

B. Scan the article on page 49 to complete these sentences.

1. World War I ended in 19___.

2. ___% of the customers in Peoria, Illinois, changed Kimberly-Clark's business plan.

The telephone, the typewriter, and the light bulb were popular new products in the late 19th century. This business magazine article is about an item that became popular after World War I—Kleenex tissues.

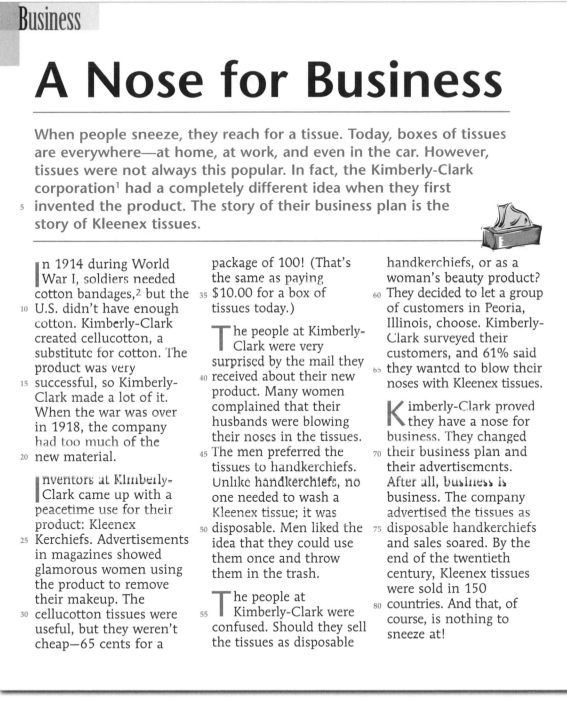

Business

A Nose for Business

When people sneeze, they reach for a tissue. Today, boxes of tissues are everywhere—at home, at work, and even in the car. However, tissues were not always this popular. In fact, the Kimberly-Clark corporation[1] had a completely different idea when they first
5   invented the product. The story of their business plan is the story of Kleenex tissues.

In 1914 during World War I, soldiers needed cotton bandages,[2] but the
10 U.S. didn't have enough cotton. Kimberly-Clark created cellucotton, a substitute for cotton. The product was very
15 successful, so Kimberly-Clark made a lot of it. When the war was over in 1918, the company had too much of the
20 new material.

Inventors at Kimberly-Clark came up with a peacetime use for their product: Kleenex
25 Kerchiefs. Advertisements in magazines showed glamorous women using the product to remove their makeup. The
30 cellucotton tissues were useful, but they weren't cheap—65 cents for a package of 100! (That's the same as paying
35 $10.00 for a box of tissues today.)

The people at Kimberly-Clark were very surprised by the mail they
40 received about their new product. Many women complained that their husbands were blowing their noses in the tissues.
45 The men preferred the tissues to handkerchiefs. Unlike handkerchiefs, no one needed to wash a Kleenex tissue; it was
50 disposable. Men liked the idea that they could use them once and throw them in the trash.

The people at
55 Kimberly-Clark were confused. Should they sell the tissues as disposable handkerchiefs, or as a woman's beauty product?
60 They decided to let a group of customers in Peoria, Illinois, choose. Kimberly-Clark surveyed their customers, and 61% said
65 they wanted to blow their noses with Kleenex tissues.

Kimberly-Clark proved they have a nose for business. They changed
70 their business plan and their advertisements. After all, business is business. The company advertised the tissues as
75 disposable handkerchiefs and sales soared. By the end of the twentieth century, Kleenex tissues were sold in 150
80 countries. And that, of course, is nothing to sneeze at!

---

[1] **corporation:** a company
[2] **bandage:** a piece of cotton cloth that covers a cut or wound on the body

8 PROCESS WHAT YOU READ

A. **Choose the correct answer to each question. Then scan the article on page 49 to check your answers.**

1. What was made from cellucotton during World War I?

    a. bandages
    b. tissues
    c. handkerchiefs

2. What is the name of the company that made tissues?

    a. Clark-Kimberly
    b. Kimberly-Clark
    c. Kleenex

3. Why were tissues popular?

    a. They were expensive.
    b. They were glamorous.
    c. They were disposable.

4. How did customers use tissues at first?

    a. to remove makeup
    b. to clean windows
    c. to blow their noses

5. Who did Kimberly-Clark survey for ideas on their product?

    a. soldiers
    b. movie stars
    c. customers

6. In how many countries can you find Kleenex tissues?

    a. 50
    b. 100
    c. 150

B. **Discuss these questions with a partner. Look back at the article to check your answers.**

1. Why are tissues better than handkerchiefs?

2. How did listening to their customers help Kimberly-Clark?

3. What does the expression "business is business" mean to you?

4. Kimberly-Clark used movie stars in its ads. Are you more interested in a product if a movie star is in the ad? Why or why not?

9   WORK WITH THE VOCABULARY

A. Choose the correct phrase to complete each sentence. Look at the words in parentheses to help you.

business is business	came up with	have a nose for
nothing to sneeze at	sales soared	substitute for

1. Cellucotton is a _____ _substitute for_ _____ cotton.
   (product similar to)

2. The inventors _____ a peace-time use for
   (thought of)
   their product.

3. Kimberly-Clark changed the use of their product because
   _____ .
   (the profit is more important than the product)

4. When Kleenex tissues were sold as disposable handkerchiefs,
   _____ .
   (people bought a lot of them)

5. Kimberly-Clark proved they _____ business.
   (are good at)

6. Kleenex tissues are sold in 150 countries, and that is
   _____ .
   (a major success)

Suffixes: -able

You can use the suffix -able to form adjectives from some verbs. For example, dispose means "to throw away or put in the trash".

dispose + -able = disposable

Disposable is an adjective that tells you an item can be thrown away.

(The -e at the end of a verb usually disappears, except after c and g.)

B. Use -able to form adjectives from the verbs below. Work with a partner to write sample sentences.

Verb	Adjective	Sample Sentence
1. dispose	_disposable_	_You can throw away disposable tissues._
2. remove	_____	_____
3. change	_____	_____
4. prefer	_____	_____
5. wash	_____	_____

A. Look at the cartoon. Discuss the questions below with your classmates.

"Talk to me, Alice. I speak woman."

1. What does the man mean when he says he speaks "woman?"

2. Do you think Alice will talk to him? Why or why not?

3. Are there differences in the way men and women think and communicate? If yes, describe the differences.

B. Put a check (✓) next to the words you know. Ask your classmates for the meanings of the words you don't know. Look up the words no one knows in a dictionary.

____ appear ____ appreciate ____ fluent ____ misunderstanding

____ respect ____ restate ____ strong ____ weakness

C. Preview the texts on pages 53 and 54 and answer these questions.

1. What is text A about?

2. What is text B about?

3. Scan the introductory material to find out Ronna Lichtenberg's job.

D. Choose one text to read. Then answer these questions.

1. What is the title of the text?

2. What do you think of when you see the word "blue"?

3. What do you think of when you see the word "pink"?

Ronna Lichtenberg is a researcher and consultant on business communications. This newspaper article discusses Lichtenberg's ideas about how different ways of thinking affect communication in the workplace.

== **Business**

Today's Business Culture:
What are they thinking?

American business culture is different than it was 30 years ago. In those days, almost all business owners, company presidents, managers, and supervisors were men. In order to succeed, women in business had to learn to think the way their male bosses thought. Ronna Lichtenberg, in her article
5 "Be Fluent in Both Pink and Blue," identifies two ways of thinking in the business world today: "blue thinking" (male) and "pink thinking" (female). Naturally, not all women "think pink" and not all men "think blue." In fact, Ms. Lichtenberg points out that most successful business people combine blue and pink thinking in their workplace communications and relationships.

10   As the chart below shows, there are important differences in pink and blue thinking styles, but Lichtenberg says neither style is "right." She also says that it's not necessary for people to change the way they think. Instead, she recommends learning to understand the two styles.

      Today in U.S. society, a boss can be a woman or a man, and half the
15 people in any company will probably have a thinking style that is different from the other half. Therefore, to be successful, workers must be able to identify and appreciate a thinking style that's different from their own.

BLUE THINKING	PINK THINKING
It's important to appear strong. People shouldn't share their weaknesses.	It's important to make connections with people. When two people talk about their weaknesses, they can form a strong connection.
20 The powerful people in a company always get respect. Workers don't tell their bosses they're wrong.	30
It's important to make friends with people who have power in a company. These 25 friendships can help improve a career.	When someone is wrong, it's important to say so. It doesn't matter if that person is the boss.
The team is more important than the individual.	35 Friendships are important. People shouldn't make friends just to help their careers.
	The team matters, but the individual is important, too.

American business leaders know that companies are successful when workers communicate well. This article discusses different communication styles in the workplace. It's based on the work of Ronna Lichtenberg, a communications consultant.

FEELING YOUR WAY (OR NOT) IN TODAY'S BUSINESS WORLD

Before 1970, men were in charge of the American business world, and most business people used the "blue style" of communication. What is the blue style? Ronna Lichtenberg, in her article "Be Fluent in Both Pink and Blue," says the "blue style" is a typical male style of communication. Is
5   there a female communication style as well? Of course! It's what Ms. Lichtenberg calls the "pink style." Lichtenberg says you should be able to use and understand both styles if you want to communicate successfully with your co-workers.

■ In the workplace, "Blues" usually
10   communicate in short, direct messages. They also have strict rules about what you should
15   and shouldn't say. One rule is: Don't talk about feelings. In fact, "Blues" rarely talk about their personal life at work. In a meeting, "Blues" prefer to talk about a task
20   they need to do and the date it's due. They don't believe it's necessary for everyone to discuss and agree on how to do the task.

■ People with a "pink style" have a
25   more informal approach to communication in the workplace. They often talk about their feelings, and they believe that conversations should begin with small talk about
30   their personal lives. In a business meeting, "Pinks" will try to get everyone to agree on how a task should be done. They think this type of consensus, or agreement, is
35   important, and they don't worry about how much time it takes.

■ In the business world, communication differences between the "Blues" and the "Pinks" can
40   sometimes create misunderstandings. Ronna Lichtenberg offers this solution: Use your own communication style to restate what you hear. For example, if you hear a brief, "blue" message
45   such as, "Everyone has to work late tonight," you can translate the message into "pink" and say: "So we have to finish the project before we can go home." If you hear a "pink"
50   message such as, "I feel bad about this, but the project is going slowly," you can restate it in "blue" by saying, "So you need more time to complete the project."

55   ■ From her research, Lichtenberg knows that "Blues" and "Pinks" are happier when they hear a message in their own style. So whether your communication style is "blue" or
60   "pink," practice restating, and you will find that the message is clear, even when the communication style is not.

13 SHARE WHAT YOU LEARNED

A. Work with a partner who read the same text.

    1. Read the focus questions for your text.

    2. Discuss the questions and write your answers.

Focus Questions for Text A

1. What's one big difference between business in the U.S. now and 30 years ago?

2. Give three examples of "blue" thinking.

3. Give three examples of "pink" thinking.

4. Why is it important to understand both types of thinking?

Focus Questions for Text B

1. Why did U.S. businesses use the "blue communication style" before 1970?

2. Describe the "pink" communication style.

3. Describe the "blue" communication style.

4. What can people with different communication styles do to prevent misunderstandings?

B. With your partner, find a pair who read a different text and form a team.

    1. Share the topic of your text with your teammates.

    2. Take turns sharing your answers to the focus questions.

    3. Add any other information from the text that you remember.

14 SHARE WHAT YOU THINK

Discuss these questions with your teammates. Then share your answers with the class.

1. Would you prefer to work for a boss with a "pink" or a "blue" communication style? Why?

2. What is your communication style? Is it the same as your teacher's style?

3. Are there different ways of thinking in different cultures? Explain.

4. Are there different ways of communicating in different cultures? Explain.

Interview

Read the questions and think about your answers. Then work in small groups to interview each other.

1. Do you believe that men and women have different communication and thinking styles? Why or why not?

2. Do you think using pink and blue to talk about communication or thinking styles is a good idea? Why or why not? Are there other colors that would be better?

3. Decide which communication style (pink or blue) is best for these situations: a) a job interview, b) a doctor's appointment, c) a date.

Chart

A. Make a chart similar to the one below. Then use the questions to survey five classmates about their opinions of different inventions, and write their responses in the chart.

- What is the most important product ever invented? Why?

- What is the worst product ever invented? Why?

THE BEST AND THE WORST INVENTIONS		
Respondent	Most Important Invention	Worst Invention
Anna	dishwasher	hand gun
Keiko	light bulb	beepers

B. Discuss the results of your survey with the class. Use the following expressions.

One out of five people thinks that . . .   *Most people think that . . .*

Write

A. Work with a partner, and list a few new popular products. Decide which of these products will be successful and why. Share your ideas with your classmates.

B. Imagine that you have invented a new product and started a company. Write a paragraph describing your product and your company. Answer some or all of these questions:

- What is your company's name? Are you a small business or a large corporation?

- What is your product's name? What does it do? Who buys it? How much does it cost? Where will you sell it?

Unit 5

Staying Healthy

In this unit you will:

- read about the ways people in the U.S. stay healthy
- learn how to understand vocabulary in context

WHAT DO YOU KNOW ABOUT STAYING HEALTHY?

A. Look at the information in the medical records. With a partner, decide who is healthier, Chad or Sam. Why? Discuss your responses with your classmates.

BARTON, CHAD

MEDICAL RECORD	
Name:	Chad Barton
Age:	25
Marital Status:	single
Address:	155 Bay Street, San Diego, CA
Occupation:	builder
Hours:	50 per week
Exercise:	3 times per week
Sleep:	4-6 hours
Notes:	very serious

HINTON, SAM

MEDICAL RECORD	
Name:	Sam Hinton
Age:	27
Marital Status:	married
Address:	645 10th Street Brooklyn, NY
Occupation:	college professor
Hours:	40 per week
Exercise:	walks dog
Sleep:	6-8 hours
Notes:	good sense of humor

B. Which of the following things do you do to stay healthy? Mark your answers with a check (✓). Discuss your responses with your classmates.

____ drink tea   ____ drink water   ____ eat fruit and vegetables

____ exercise   ____ sleep well   ____ take time to relax

____ take vitamins   ____ other _____

A. **Read the ad and answer the questions below. Share your responses with your classmates.**

Now You Can Lose Weight
with the ***Pounds-Away***
secret!

Simply take one *Pounds Away* tablet before each meal and drink 3–4 glasses of water. That's all there is to it. Within two weeks you will notice a slimmer, more attractive person looking back at you from the mirror.

ORDER YOUR FREE SAMPLE OF *POUNDS AWAY* TODAY.

1. Do you know any people who have lost weight using this kind of product?

2. Do you think this advertisement is telling the truth? Why or why not?

B. **Guess the meanings of the words in the box and choose the word that best completes each sentence. Check your guesses after you read the article on page 60.**

effective	ingredients	miracle	painless	secret

1. I have a special product to show you. Don't tell anyone, it's a _____.

2. The product contains water, alcohol, and sugar. These _____ make it work quickly.

3. You won't believe how quickly it works. It's a _____.

4. Don't worry, it won't hurt. The treatment is _____.

5. This product will help you feel better right away. It's very

_____.

C. **Put a check (✓) next to the words you know. Ask your classmates for the meanings of the words you don't know. Look up the words no one knows in a dictionary.**

____ cure (*n.,v.*)   ____ false   ____ formula

____ lie (*v.*)   ____ phony   ____ prove

2 BUILDING READING SKILLS: Finding Clues in Context

> **Finding clues in context** means getting information about the meaning of important words in a text by looking at the sentences nearby. You will usually find the clues in the same sentence or paragraph as the important words. These clues can be synonyms (similar words), definitions, examples, or contrasts (opposite ideas or words).

Practice Finding Clues in Context

Read the paragraph and think about the meanings of the underlined words. Use context clues to answer the questions below.

> *Many people get _migraines_. These headaches make them very ill. To help their patients, doctors are studying the _causes_ of migraines. They know there are many reasons for these headaches. _Some things in the environment_ can cause a migraine. Poor air quality, lights, or too much noise in homes and workplaces can result in a migraine attack. Some doctors believe, however, that the _emotional_ (not the physical) _environment_ is a more likely cause of an attack.*

1. What is a migraine? (Look for a synonym.)

2. What does *causes* mean? (Look for the definition.)

3. What are *things in the environment*? (Look for examples.)

4. What do you think the *emotional environment* is? (Look for a contrast clue.)

Use Your Reading Skills

A. Preview the introductory material, the title, and the headings of the article on page 60. Discuss these questions with your classmates.

   1. What is the topic of this article?

   2. What do you know about this topic?

B. As you read the article on page 60, highlight the clues that tell you the meanings of these words. Then write the clues on the lines below.

   1. quack _____

   2. quick fix _____

   3. urban population _____

   4. opium _____

   5. radium _____

   6. illegal _____

Medical quackery is false, or phony, medicine. Unfortunately, it is alive and well in the U.S. This article from an educational journal talks about quackery, past and present.

The Painful Truth About the Painless Cure: Medical Quackery in the United States

THE MEDICINE SHOW

Quacks, or phony doctors, were very common in the United States in the 1800s and early 1900s. They put on "medicine shows," where the audience watched someone dance or sing until the "doctor" came on stage. The quack
5 told the audience he had a medicine that would take care of all their medical problems. To make the audience believe him, the quack always asked someone in the audience to try the "medicine." That person (who secretly worked for the quack) drank some, and after a few seconds shouted out, "I'm cured!" This made the medicine seem like a fast and easy cure—a quick fix—so
10 people bought bottle after bottle.

QUACKERY'S SUCCESS

Quackery flourished[1] in the United States from the 1860s to the 1920s because of the growth of the urban population—more and more people were moving to the cities. This meant that diseases could spread quickly from
15 person to person. People were scared, so they bought anything they thought would protect or cure them.

THE DANGERS

In most cases, quacks' medicines were only dangerous because people took them instead of going to real doctors. Sometimes, however, the medicines
20 were deadly. Quacks added ingredients such as opium (a powerful drug) and radium (a radioactive element) to their bottles. Some people got sicker after taking the medicine, and some people died. Of course, the quacks took no responsibility for the deaths. They said, "Well, the medicine worked for awhile, but poor so-and-so was just too sick."

25 ## GOVERNMENT ACTION

It took many years for the U.S. government to take strong action against quacks. Finally in 1938, the Federal Food, Drug, and Cosmetic Act made it illegal to sell a false medicine or lie about its ingredients. That made quackery against the law. By the early 1960s, all drug manufacturers had to
30 prove that their products were safe and effective.

(continued)

[1]**flourish:** to grow, to be successful

QUACKERY TODAY

In the 21st century the quacks look different, but they're selling the same "quick fix." There are advertisements everywhere that promise fast, easy ways to lose weight, gain weight, grow hair, or become more attractive. Government
35 health agencies warn Americans about products that advertise a "Painless Cure," or a "Secret Formula," but many people don't pay attention. They'll try anything that says it will help them feel or look better. That's why, sadly, as long as there are people who sell these phony medicines, there will always be people to buy them.

4 PROCESS WHAT YOU READ

A. Form groups of four and assign one question to each person. Write the answer to your question on your own. Then share your answers in your groups.

1. Who put on medicine shows and what did they do during these shows?

2. How did the growth of cities help quackery flourish?

3. What did the U.S. government do to protect people?

4. Is quackery dead in the U.S. today? Explain why or why not.

B. Discuss your answers to these questions with your classmates.

1. Why do you think quacks used medicine shows to sell their medicine?

2. Why do you think so many people believe in a "quick fix"?

3. How can you protect yourself from quackery?

5 WORK WITH THE VOCABULARY

Match the words with the phrases that define them. Look back at the article to check your answers.

___ 1. cure (v.)	a. something that must not be known by other people
___ 2. deadly	b. substances you need to make a medication
___ 3. ingredients	c. to make someone healthy again
___ 4. painful	d. likely to cause death
___ 5. phony	e. causing pain
___ 6. secret	f. not real

6 GET READY TO READ ABOUT: Stress

A. Answer the survey questions below. Then survey nine other classmates. Use tick marks (卌) to record all the *yes* or *no* answers.

Managing Stress	Yes	No
1. Do you exercise regularly?		
2. Do you get 7–9 hours of sleep each night?		
3. Do you spend a lot of time sitting?		
4. Do you eat fruits and vegetables?		
5. Do you drink several glasses of water every day?		
6. Do you drink a lot of coffee?		
7. Do you eat foods high in sugar?		
8. Do you meditate or do yoga?		

B. Discuss the results of the survey with the class. Use the following expressions:

Nine out of ten people . . .   *Only a few people . . .*

A majority of people . . .   *Most people . . .*

A minority of people . . .   *Some people . . .*

Use Your Reading Skills

A. Preview the article on page 63. Then predict which of the following ideas you'll find in the article. Check your predictions after you read the article.

____ 1. causes of stress

____ 2. why stress can be good for you

____ 3. how stress affects children

____ 4. how stress affects the human body

____ 5. ways to reduce stress

____ 6. why famous people have stress

B. As you read the article on page 63, highlight the clues that tell you the meanings of these words. Then write the clues on the lines below.

1. traumatic events   _____

2. unmanageable   _____

3. survive   _____

4. flee   _____

One of the most talked about health issues in the U.S. is stress. This website article defines stress and gives suggestions for reducing it in daily life.

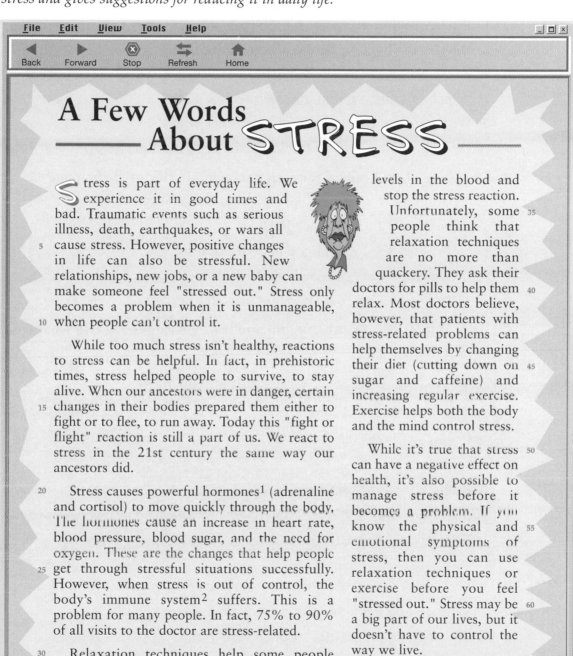

File   Edit   View   Tools   Help

◀ Back   ▶ Forward   ⊗ Stop   ⇄ Refresh   🏠 Home

A Few Words About STRESS

Stress is part of everyday life. We experience it in good times and bad. Traumatic events such as serious illness, death, earthquakes, or wars all
5 cause stress. However, positive changes in life can also be stressful. New relationships, new jobs, or a new baby can make someone feel "stressed out." Stress only becomes a problem when it is unmanageable,
10 when people can't control it.

While too much stress isn't healthy, reactions to stress can be helpful. In fact, in prehistoric times, stress helped people to survive, to stay alive. When our ancestors were in danger, certain
15 changes in their bodies prepared them either to fight or to flee, to run away. Today this "fight or flight" reaction is still a part of us. We react to stress in the 21st century the same way our ancestors did.

20 Stress causes powerful hormones[1] (adrenaline and cortisol) to move quickly through the body. The hormones cause an increase in heart rate, blood pressure, blood sugar, and the need for oxygen. These are the changes that help people
25 get through stressful situations successfully. However, when stress is out of control, the body's immune system[2] suffers. This is a problem for many people. In fact, 75% to 90% of all visits to the doctor are stress-related.

30 Relaxation techniques help some people reduce stress. Deep breathing, muscle relaxation, and meditation can actually decrease hormone levels in the blood and stop the stress reaction. Unfortunately, some
35 people think that relaxation techniques are no more than quackery. They ask their doctors for pills to help them
40 relax. Most doctors believe, however, that patients with stress-related problems can help themselves by changing their diet (cutting down on
45 sugar and caffeine) and increasing regular exercise. Exercise helps both the body and the mind control stress.

While it's true that stress
50 can have a negative effect on health, it's also possible to manage stress before it becomes a problem. If you know the physical and
55 emotional symptoms of stress, then you can use relaxation techniques or exercise before you feel "stressed out." Stress may be
60 a big part of our lives, but it doesn't have to control the way we live.

Adapted from the National Women's Health Resource website

[1] **hormone:** a chemical in the body
[2] **immune system:** the body's way of fighting illness

8 PROCESS WHAT YOU READ

A. **Read the questions. Use the underlined words to help you scan the article on page 63 for the answers. Highlight your answers and check with a partner.**

1. When does stress become a <u>problem</u>?

2. What is the <u>fight or flight</u> reaction?

3. What <u>changes</u> in the body happen because of stress?

4. Which <u>relaxation techniques</u> help reduce stress?

5. What types of changes in <u>diet</u> can reduce stress?

6. Why should we learn to recognize the <u>symptoms of stress</u>?

B. **Choose the best heading for each paragraph in the article on page 63.**

_d_ Paragraph 1	a. What Happens to the Body
___ Paragraph 2	b. Just Relax!
___ Paragraph 3	c. Keep It Under Control
___ Paragraph 4	d. Stress is Normal
___ Paragraph 5	e. The Fight or Flight Reaction

C. **Look at the lists of most stressful and least stressful jobs. Use what you learned from the article and your own experience to answer the questions below.**

WHICH JOB DO YOU WANT?	
A. Five Most Stressful Jobs	**B. Five Least Stressful Jobs**
1. President of the United States	1. Medical records technician
2. Firefighter	2. Janitor
3. Senior corporate executive	3. Forklift operator
4. Race car driver	4. Musical instrument repairer
5. Taxi driver	5. Florist

Source: *Jobs Rated Almanac*

1. Why do you think the jobs in list A are extremely stressful?

2. Why do you think the jobs in list B are less stressful?

3. Did any jobs on the lists surprise you? Why?

4. Would you add any jobs to list A or B? Which ones? Why?

D. **Discuss the questions below with a partner.**

1. What are the top three causes of stress in your life?

2. How do you respond to a stressful situation?

3. What kinds of things do you do to reduce stress?

A. Match the words below with their antonyms (opposites).

____ **1.** quickly		a. pleasant
____ **2.** increase		b. relaxed
____ **3.** unmanageable		c. slowly
____ **4.** flee		d. decrease
____ **5.** traumatic		e. stay
____ **6.** stressed out		f. manageable

Prefixes: *un-*

The prefix *un-* means "not." You can add *un-* to certain adjectives to create the opposite or antonym of the original adjective.

For example, *manageable* means "easy to manage or control."

** *un-* + manageable = unmanageable**

Unmanageable is the opposite of *manageable*. It means "not easy to manage or control."

B. Use *un-* to form new adjectives from the words below. Work with a partner to write sample sentences.

Adjective	*un-* + Adjective	Sample Sentence
1. manageable	unmanageable	My workload is unmanageable.
2. safe	_____	_____
3. successful	_____	_____
4. attractive	_____	_____
5. important	_____	_____

C. Rewrite the paragraph replacing the underlined words with these words.

unbelievable	unhappy	unhealthy	uninterested	unmanageable	unwell

It's <u>hard to believe</u> that today, some people are <u>not interested</u> in learning about stress. Perhaps they think stress is just <u>not manageable</u>. They certainly know that stress is <u>not healthy</u>. Sometimes these people go to the doctor because they're <u>not well</u> or <u>not happy</u>. Doctors can often help people learn to control stress.

It's unbelievable that today . . .

A. **Look at the cartoon. Discuss the questions below with your classmates.**

"Hi. My name is Barry, and I check my E-mail
two to three hundred times a day."

1. What are these people doing?

2. What is Barry's problem?

3. Is it serious? Why or why not?

4. Do you have email? If yes, how often do you check it?

B. **Put a check (✓) next to the words you know. Ask your classmates for the meanings of the words you don't know. Look up the words no one knows in a dictionary.**

____ affect   ____ alcoholic

____ effect   ____ encourage

____ fun   ____ immune system

____ jokes   ____ laughter

C. **Preview the texts on pages 67 and 68 and answer these questions.**

1. What is the topic of each text?

2. What do you know about these topics?

D. **Choose one text to read. Then answer these questions.**

1. What is the title of the text?

2. What do you predict you will learn?

When some people have problems, they go to a support group to talk to people with similar problems. This newspaper article talks about different kinds of support groups.

HealthNews

A LOOK AT . . . Support Groups

Every day, all over the United States, people with serious problems look for help. They often find it in support groups, places ₅ where people with similar problems offer understanding, information, and advice.

These groups may meet in churches, in community ₁₀ centers, in health clinics, or on the Internet. The reasons for starting a support group may be different, but the results are the same: people ₁₅ help each other.

The most famous support group in the world began in 1935, in Akron, Ohio when two men met and talked about their experiences with alcohol. ₂₀ Bill was a recovering alcoholic[1], and Bob was an alcoholic who wanted to stop drinking. Whenever Bob got depressed, Bill encouraged him not to drink. With Bill's support, Bob ₂₅ stopped drinking and stayed sober. This was the beginning of Alcoholics Anonymous or AA. In an AA meeting, members come together to share their experiences and fight their ₃₀ need for alcohol or drugs. AA has over two million members all over the world, and it's the model for many other support groups.

AA is a support group that helps ₃₅ people with alcoholism, but there are other groups for almost every type of disease or medical condition. Doctors or nurses usually start support groups, but patients often ₄₀ run the group. In these groups, members talk to one another about their symptoms, treatments, and feelings. (There are also support ₄₅ groups for the families of people who are ill.)

Not everyone who needs a support group can get to the meetings. In that case the ₅₀ Internet makes it possible for people to join online support groups. Chat rooms and e-mail allow people to connect with group members from other communities. Many people log ₅₅ on to these sites because they can get support day or night. Online groups also appeal to shy people. They can read what other people have to say about a particular ₆₀ medical problem, but they don't have to speak up.

Whether online, in a church basement, at a community center, or a health clinic, members of support ₆₅ groups get the comfort[2] they need. They can talk freely about frustrations[3] and fears, and, sometimes, it's a place to find hope. Support group members discover one ₇₀ fact that can make a huge difference in their lives—they are not alone.

---

[1] **recovering alcoholic:** someone who has an addiction to alcohol, but no longer drinks it
[2] **comfort:** a feeling of being physically relaxed and satisfied
[3] **frustration:** a feeling of anger or dissatisfaction because you cannot do what you want to do

Some medical researchers in the U.S. study the connection between laughter and good health. This magazine article discusses what the research shows.

Laughing Your Way to Health

Michael Lao

Do you remember the last time you had a really good laugh? Were you watching a funny TV show or listening to a good joke? Were you
5 sharing funny stories with friends? Did you know that laughter can help your immune system? It's even possible that with each laugh, you reduce your chance of getting a cold or having an
10 allergy attack. In fact, if you laugh before you go to bed, you'll probably have a very good night's sleep.

Some medical professionals believe that laughing is an excellent
15 way to stay healthy and relieve pain. Stress hormones have a negative effect on the heart. Some studies show that laughter reduces these stress hormones in the body. Thanks to this research,
20 many doctors think that laughter can help keep a heart healthy.

Roxanne Karnes is a cancer-research nurse. She uses laughter to help patients live with their pain. She
25 says that laughter improves the quality of life for her patients, their families, and the doctors and nurses who help them. Dr. Clifford Kuhn is a professor of psychiatry,
30 a professional comedian, and a public speaker. He studies how laughter affects mental and physical health. Dr. Kuhn says that laughter is good for the body
35 because it creates new cells and helps create antibodies[1] that fight off disease.

The medical research on laughter and the desire to get well and stay
40 well is making more and more Americans use laughter to feel better. There are more than eighty laughter clubs across the country and many laughter classes in medical centers and
45 cancer clinics. People join these clubs and classes not to tell jokes, but to learn exercises that will help them laugh. Club members may walk around like penguins[2] or make silly,
50 childish faces at one another. The idea is to have fun. When things are fun, it's easier to smile and laugh.

Alan Klein, author of The Healing Power of Humor, says that
55 we all need to laugh, especially at ourselves. To develop our "humor skills," we need to see the humor in our own actions and reactions. With practice we can get better at this.
60 Klein offers this advice to those who have a hard time laughing when they're feeling low: "If you can't laugh, smile. If you can't smile, fake a smile[3]. Do this enough, and you will soon think
65 of things worth smiling about."

---

[1] **antibodies:** part of the immune system; cells in the body that fight infection
[2] **penguin:** a black and white seabird that lives in the Antarctic
[3] **fake a smile:** to pretend to smile when you don't feel like smiling

13 SHARE WHAT YOU LEARNED

A. Work with a partner who read the same text.

1. Read the focus questions for your text.

2. Discuss the questions and write your answers.

Focus Questions for Text A

1. What is a support group?

2. Why do people go to these groups?

3. What is the most famous support group? How did it start?

4. What are some other kinds of support groups?

Focus Questions for Text B

1. What medical problems can laughter help relieve?

2. How does laughter affect the body?

3. Why are people joining laughter clubs or classes?

4. What do people do in these clubs or classes?

B. With your partner, find a pair who read a different text and form a team.

1. Share the topic of your text with your teammates.

2. Take turns sharing your answers to the focus questions.

3. Add any other information from the text that you remember.

14 SHARE WHAT YOU THINK

Discuss these questions with your teammates. Then share your answers with the class.

1. Do you think support groups are a good idea? Why or why not?

2. Do you believe that laughter is good medicine? Why or why not?

3. Do you think it's a good idea to smile when you don't feel like smiling? Why or why not?

4. How do you help your friends and family members when they're ill or going through a difficult time?

15 REFLECT ON WHAT YOU READ IN THIS UNIT

Interview

Read the questions and think about your answers. Then interview a partner. With your partner, find one thing that makes both of you laugh.

1. How often do you laugh? All the time? Sometimes? Rarely?

2. Do you like to listen to jokes? Why or why not?

3. What makes you laugh?

Chart

A. Work in small groups. Think of two positive, two negative, and two interesting things about Internet support groups. Look at the statements in the chart. Write your ideas in each section of the chart.

INTERNET SUPPORT GROUPS		
Positive	**Negative**	**Interesting**
You can meet with people at any time of the day or night.	You can't be sure who you're talking to.	You can wear your pajamas to a meeting and no one will know.

B. Share your charts with the other groups. Tell your classmates whether you think Internet support groups are a good idea or not. Use the ideas in your chart to support your opinion.

Write

A. Work with a partner and brainstorm a list of things that can cause stress.

B. Write a paragraph that answers some or all of these questions:

- Is the U.S. a stressful place to live? Why or why not?

- Do you feel that people in the U.S. are more stressed out than other people in the world? Why or why not?

- How do you respond to stress?

- What advice do you have for people who are stressed out?

Unit 6

One of a Kind

In this unit you will:

● read about the importance of the individual in U.S. culture
● learn how to infer meaning in a text

DO YOU THINK INDIVIDUALITY IS IMPORTANT?

A. Look at the cartoon. How is Wilson different from his co-workers?
Imagine you are one of the people at the table. How do you feel?
Imagine you are Wilson. How do you feel? Discuss your responses with
your classmates.

"Wilson is our most original thinker
- I want everyone to think like him."

B. Think about these statements and tell your classmates whether you agree
or disagree. Give examples that support your opinions.

1. In sports, the team is more important than individual players.

2. Sports teams only do well if they have great players.

3. At work, the person who is "one of a kind," or different from everyone
else, is usually more successful.

A. **Read the sentences. Underline the word or phrase that defines or explains the circled word or phrase. Check your answers after you read the essay on pages 74–75.**

1. Individuality, or the qualities that make one person different from another, is very important in American culture.

2. An individual may be a member of a group, but it's important to think of him or her as a separate person as well.

3. When one group stereotypes another group, they make general statements that are untrue. For example, if they see one lazy student, they might say *all* students are lazy.

4. Stereotyping leads to prejudice, when one person's negative opinion of a group of people is based on their race, age, religion, or gender.

5. For more than 200 years, Americans kept Africans in slavery, forcing them to work without pay and selling them as property. Slavery officially ended on January 1, 1863.

6. In the 20th century, many women experienced job discrimination. They often couldn't get the same jobs as males and when they did, they were frequently paid less.

7. U.S. laws protect citizens' civil rights. For example, male and female citizens of all ages, races, and religions have the right to vote, say what they think, and get fair and equal treatment by the government.

8. Ageism has become a widespread problem in the U.S. Some people think of older people as problems rather than as valuable and productive members of society.

9. Although it is necessary to conform to, or obey, certain standards of conduct, it is important to be your own person as well.

10. People from various ethnic groups live in the United States. These groups represent different races, nations, tribes, and regions.

B. **Discuss these questions with your classmates.**

1. Who are some famous American individuals? Why are they famous?

2. What are some stereotypes about Americans?

3. What are some of the qualities that make you different from other people?

4. Have you ever experienced prejudice? How did you feel?

5. Do you know places in the world where prejudice is a very big problem?

6. Do you know your civil rights? What are they?

2 BUILDING READING SKILLS: Inferring

> Writers don't always state all their ideas directly in a text. Sometimes you have to **infer**, or figure out, some information. To infer, you connect what you read in the text with what you already know. This is sometimes called reading between the lines.

Practice Inferring

Read the paragraphs and infer the answers to the questions.

> Peter Pitchlynn was a member of the Native American tribe called the Choctaw Nation. During his lifetime, Pitchlynn spoke out against discrimination and prejudice toward Native Americans. In the 1850s, he made many trips to Washington. During these trips, Pitchlynn talked about Native American rights with everyone he met, including Abraham Lincoln.

1. Is Peter Pitchlynn alive today?
2. Why did Pitchlynn go to Washington and not Los Angeles?
3. Do you think Pitchlynn's work in Washington was easy?

> Sojourner Truth was born a slave, but she ran away to be free. She couldn't read or write, but she was very intelligent and had a beautiful voice. She traveled around the northern U.S. telling stories about her life and singing songs against slavery. She spoke out for civil rights and women's rights until her death.

4. Why do you think Sojourner Truth couldn't read or write?
5. Why did she tell stories about her life?
6. Do you think Sojourner Truth was a brave woman? Why? Why not?

Use Your Reading Skills

A. **Preview the essay on pages 74–75. Discuss these questions with your classmates.**
   1. What is the topic of the essay?
   2. What do you already know about this topic?

B. **With a partner, predict what you will learn about these topics. Then check your predictions as you read the essay.**
   a. American children
   b. prejudice and discrimination in the U.S.

This essay talks about the rights and the importance of the individual in U.S. culture.

The Value of the Individual

Experts on U.S. culture today often note that most Americans identify themselves as individuals first, and then as members of various groups. In fact, most Americans believe that the freedom to be an individual is their birthright.[1] The U.S. Constitution and legal system both support individual freedom. They protect each person's right to fair and equal treatment at school, at work, and in the community. Discrimination against an individual because of gender, age, race, or religion is illegal.

In U.S. society, even young children learn to be individuals. They make choices and give their opinions almost from the time they begin talking. Adults ask young people to conform to, or follow, certain standards of behavior (being polite, offering to help others), but they also tell them not to give up their individuality just to fit in with, or be a part of, a group.

The power of the individual is a theme[2] in most U.S. history books. Students learn about men and women who influenced or changed American society for the better. These famous people belonged to a variety of ethnic groups (Native American, African-American, Latino, Asian, Eastern European, etc.). Many of them came from families without money or power, and they often believed in unpopular ideas. They advocated, or spoke out in support of, basic human rights, and they spoke out against stereotypes. Peter Pitchlynn (advocate for Native American rights), Sojourner Truth (anti-slavery and civil rights activist), Elizabeth Cady Stanton (advocate for women's right to vote), and Cesar Chavez (farm workers' rights advocate) are just a few examples.

From childhood, Americans learn to believe in an ideal[3] society where people respect individual differences. This idea, however, often contrasts with the reality. Unfortunately, there are still people who stereotype members of other groups, rather than think of them as individuals. There is still racism (prejudice toward people of color), ageism (prejudice towards older people), and gender discrimination.

Teachers, civil rights workers, and lawyers actively fight against

---

[1] **birthright:** a basic right, something you have from the moment you are born
[2] **theme:** a subject, an idea
[3] **ideal:** exactly right, perfect

racism, ageism, and sexism. They
see them as enemies[4] of individuality, and they speak out against
them—in classrooms, in court-
rooms, and anywhere people will
listen. Thanks to these advocates,
equality remains a powerful
principle in U.S. culture. Belief in
equality for every individual is a
strong weapon[5] in the fight against
discrimination and prejudice in
American society.

[4] **enemy:** someone who hates you and wants to harm you or stop you from being successful
[5] **weapon:** something you use to fight with

4 PROCESS WHAT YOU READ

A. Answer the questions. Look back at the essay to check your answers.

1. How do Americans identify themselves?

2. How do children in the U.S. learn about individuality?

3. Name some of the famous Americans in the essay. What did they do?

4. What are the enemies of individuality and who fights against them?

B. Choose the best heading for each paragraph in the essay.

____ Paragraph 1   a. Individuals Who Made a Difference in Society

____ Paragraph 2   b. The Ideal Is Not Quite Real

____ Paragraph 3   c. Individual Freedom Is an American Birthright

____ Paragraph 4   d. The Fight Against Discrimination Continues

____ Paragraph 5   e. It's Never Too Early to Be an Individual

C. Work in a small group. Read the ideas from the essay and infer the answers to the questions.

IDEAS	QUESTIONS
1. Most Americans identify themselves as individuals first, and then as members of various groups.	What groups is the author talking about?
2. Children make choices and give their opinions almost from the time they begin talking.	Give some examples of the choices children make.
3. Many famous Americans came from families without money or power.	What does this tell you about U.S. culture?
4. Teachers, civil rights workers, and lawyers actively fight against all kinds of discrimination.	Why are these people the ones who fight discrimination?

5 WORK WITH THE VOCABULARY

A. Choose the word or phrase that has a meaning similar to each word or phrase.
Then scan the essay on pages 74–75 to check your answers.

1. fit in with

    a. be a part of
    b. wear nice clothes

2. speak out

    a. say nothing
    b. say what you think

3. conform

    a. follow
    b. win

4. influence (*v.*)

    a. change
    b. enter

5. advocate for (*v.*)

    a. read about
    b. support

6. fair

    a. equal
    b. right

B. Replace the underlined phrases in each statement below with these words
or phrases.

a. fight

b. ageism

c. contrasts with

d. give their opinions

e. give up

f. racism

g. remains

h. speak out against

_____ **1.** American teenagers sometimes <u>don't keep</u> their individuality when they're part of a group.

_____ **2.** American parents want their children to be polite, but they also want them to <u>say what they think</u>.

_____ **3.** The ideal society <u>is different from</u> reality, because some people don't respect individuality.

_____ **4.** It's important to <u>act against</u> discrimination in all areas of American society.

_____ **5.** <u>Discrimination on the basis of race</u> is illegal in the U.S., but it continues to be a problem.

_____ **6.** In today's society, people are no longer afraid to <u>publicly criticize</u> racism.

_____ **7.** According to advocates for senior citizens' rights, <u>prejudice towards older people</u> is still a problem in the U.S.

_____ **8.** Equality <u>continues to be</u> an important principle in American society and culture.

A. Work with a partner. Look at the cartoon and discuss whether these people are unique (special) or odd (strange).

B. Discuss these questions with your classmates.

1. Do you know any unique people? What makes them unique?

2. Do you enjoy reading or hearing about odd people? Why or why not?

3. Describe the oddest person you know.

Use Your Reading Skills

Preview the article on pages 78–79 to answer these questions. Check your answers after you read the article.

1. What was Robert Ripley's profession?

    a. athlete   b. cartoonist   c. movie star

2. What kind of person was he?

    a. ordinary   b. unusual   c. boring

3. Did he like to travel?

    a. yes, a lot   b. yes, a little   c. no, not at all

4. Was he successful?

    a. no, not at all   b. yes, a little   c. yes, very

This is a short biography of cartoonist Robert Ripley. He was a unique individual whose interest in odd people and things perfectly matched the interests of his fellow Americans.

File   Edit   View   Tools   Help

◄ Back   ► Forward   ⊗ Stop   ⇄ Refresh   🏠 Home

Believe it or not, it pays to be *Odd!*

Robert Leroy Ripley, an artist, author, and radio broadcaster, was born on Christmas Day, 1893, in Santa Rosa, California. A talented but shy, self-taught artist, Ripley sold his first drawing to *Life* magazine when he was only 14. At the age of 20, Ripley drew cartoons for the sports
5 pages of the *San Francisco Chronicle*. Four years later, after he moved to New York, Ripley became the sports cartoonist for the *New York Globe*.

In 1918, Ripley created his first collection of cartoons that described odd or
10 unusual things some athletes did, such as losing 22 pounds in one baseball game or running 500 yards backwards in 14 seconds. Ripley's editor at the *Globe* wanted a title for the cartoon that showed
15 how amazing this true information was. After much deliberation,[1] they chose the title: *Believe It or Not!*—and the cartoon was an instant success.

Robert Ripley visited 198 countries
20 during his career, but he felt most at home in China. He thought Chinese culture was fascinating. When he had parties, he often greeted his guests in traditional Chinese silk robes. He made elaborate[2] dinners and told his guests exactly how each dish was prepared. He was so taken[3] with Chinese culture that for a while he even
25 signed his cartoons "Rip Li!"

People knew Ripley as a strange man who loved strange things. He drew his cartoons every day from 7 A.M. to 11 A.M.—upside down! He dressed in bright colors and patterns and wore big bowties. He collected cars but never learned to drive. A nonswimmer, he owned a collection of
30 boats, including dug-out canoes and a Chinese sailing junk.

The 1930s and 1940s were the Golden Age of Ripley. The phrase "Believe It or Not!" was a part of everyday speech. In small towns across

---

[1] **deliberation:** a thoughtful discussion
[2] **elaborate:** carefully planned and made up of many parts
[3] **be taken with something:** to find something attractive or interesting

the United States, people filled halls and theaters to hear his lectures and see his films. Later, he had his own television show where he introduced his wonders to the world.

Robert Ripley found success by writing and drawing about unique and unusual people. Although he was from a small town, self-taught, and shy, Ripley became a famous public figure. By the time he died in 1949, he had honorary titles and degrees from several universities, he was a millionaire, and he owned his own island. Believe it or not!

8 PROCESS WHAT YOU READ

Read each sentence and decide what information you can infer. Choose the correct answer.

Read	Infer
1. Ripley sold his first drawing to *Life* magazine when he was only 14.	a. Magazines often buy drawings from 14-year-olds. (b.) At 14, he was as talented as an adult artist.
2. He made elaborate dinners and told his guests exactly how each dish was prepared.	a. He was a cooking teacher. b. He liked to explain things.
3. He dressed in bright colors and patterns and wore big bow ties.	a. He wanted people to notice him. b. He didn't like people to look at him.
4. He owned a collection of boats including dug-out canoes and a Chinese sailing junk.	a. He collected boats and garbage. b. A Chinese junk is a boat.
5. In small towns across the U.S., people filled halls and theaters to hear his lectures and see his films.	a. Ripley traveled all over the U.S. b. Ripley listened to many lectures.

9 WORK WITH THE VOCABULARY

Cross out the word that does not belong in each word set.

1. amazing   wonderful   ordinary   surprising

2. similar   strange   different   unusual

3. fascinating   interesting   exciting   boring

4. unique   one of a kind   typical   special

A. Read the descriptions of the people who have received the Medal of Freedom and answer the questions below.

> Every year, the president of the United States gives the Medal of Freedom to individuals whose lives and work serve or served American society. Among honorees of this prestigious award are:
>
> ❖ a baseball player who fought prejudice to achieve his success
> ❖ a TV entertainer who used his program to improve race relations
> ❖ a newspaper editor who fights discrimination
> ❖ the creator and host of a children's educational TV show
> ❖ a doctor with the World Health Organization
> ❖ a world-famous opera singer and conductor
> ❖ the founder of a major technology company
> ❖ First Lady of the United States

1. What can you infer about the people who get the Medal of Freedom?

2. If you could give the Medal of Freedom to only three of the people listed above, who would you choose? Why?

3. Imagine you are the President. Which famous person will you give the medal to this year?

B. Put a check (✓) next to the words and phrases you know. Ask your classmates for the meanings of the ones you don't know. Look up the words and phrases no one knows in a dictionary.

____ publish   ____ full moon   ____ hardworking

____ in charge   ____ volunteer   ____ uneducated

C. Preview the texts on pages 81 and 82.

1. Who are these texts about?

2. Why are these people important?

D. Choose one text to read. Then complete these statements.

1. The title of my text is . . .

2. The topic of the text is . . .

3. His/Her occupation was . . .

This is an excerpt from a biography of Cora Wilson Stewart (1875–1958). She was an educator who came up with the idea of the "Moonlight Schools"— literacy classes for adults.

A Walk in the Moonlight

On the night of September 5, 1911, a full moon lit the roads of Rowan County, Kentucky. By the light of the moon, men and women, from 18 to 86 years old, walked down from the mountains and out of the forests into 50 schoolhouses. During the day, children sat in these one-room schoolhouses and learned to read and write.

5   On that September night, however, the schools were filled with adults who couldn't read or write anything, even their own names. They came to the "moonlight school" because one woman, Cora Wilson Stewart, told them they could learn—and they believed her.

Born in 1875 in Rowan County, Kentucky, Cora Stewart was an intelligent

10   young educator who traveled to all the schools in her county. She knew that literacy, the ability to read and write, was a key to success. She discovered, however, that many of the hard working, uneducated parents of the children couldn't read the letters that came in the mail or the daily newspaper. They asked Mrs. Stewart for help.

Mrs. Stewart asked several teachers if they would volunteer to teach reading

15   and writing to adults. All the teachers agreed. They talked to people all over the county about the "moonlight school." On the first night, the teachers expected 150 people to come to school; instead there were over 1,200 people! From that night on, the moonlight school changed people's lives.

Cora Stewart believed that adults needed to read and write about things that

20   interested them, so she prepared special materials. She wrote simple stories about life on the farm and in the mountains, and she published an easy-to-read newspaper. She also taught the students to write their names. Instead of using chalkboards, the teachers wrote each name on a pad of soft paper so that the students could feel the shape of the letters. Then they traced, or copied, the letters over and over with a

25   pencil until they could write their names on their own. One of the most exciting moments in any class was when someone shouted out his or her name and held it up high in the air.

Mrs. Stewart called that first school night in 1911 "the brightest

30   moonlit night the world has ever seen." Thanks to her, the moonlight schools helped hundreds of people step out of the darkness. For the people of Rowan County (and eventually for people all

35   across the United States), Cora Wilson Stewart was one of education's brightest stars.

This brief biography of Walt Whitman (1819–1892), an American poet, talks about Whitman's early years and his first book of poetry, Leaves of Grass.

WALT WHITMAN: Poet of the People

Walt Whitman, one of America's most famous poets, was born on May 31, 1819 on Long Island in New York. Whitman's father was hard-working, but he wasn't able to make a good living as a carpenter or a farmer in
5 New York. When Walt was 14, his family moved away and he stayed in the city. This experience gave Whitman the strong sense of independence he had all his life.

Whitman had many different jobs. He was an office boy, a printer, a teacher, a newspaper journalist, a short
10 story writer, a newspaper editor, and a house builder. Even though Whitman's formal education ended when he was 11, he wasn't an uneducated man. New York was his classroom. He visited museums to study art, history, and archeology, and he went to plays and concerts to learn about drama and music.

15 No one knew that Whitman was a poet until 1885, when at the age of 36, he published his first book of poetry, *Leaves of Grass*. In one of the poems in the book, "Crossing Brooklyn Ferry," Whitman tells how he felt when he took a boat across the river from Brooklyn to Manhattan. Here are a few lines:

> *I loved well those cities;*
> 20 *I loved well the stately*[1] *and rapid river;*
> *The men and women I saw were all near to me*[2]

These lines show how different Whitman's poetry was from the popular poetry of his time. It didn't rhyme.[3] It wasn't about exotic, faraway places. Instead he wrote about American cities and farmlands, and he celebrated the people and
25 everyday events of American life.

Whitman was different in other ways as well. Poets of his time were usually men in their 20s who came from wealthy[4] families. They had little work experience, and they dressed in fancy clothes. By contrast, Whitman's photo in *Leaves of Grass* shows a 36-year-old man in workman's clothes.

30 The response to Whitman's work was mixed: some people loved it, some hated it. Many critics didn't understand this new type of poetry. However, Ralph Waldo Emerson, a famous American writer, urged Whitman to continue. "I greet you at the beginning of a great career," he wrote.

Whitman believed that his poetry was different from traditional poetry, in
35 the same way that American society was different from traditional societies. The power of American society came from its people, not from its leaders. Whitman said, "The United States themselves are . . . the greatest poem." For many Americans, Walt Whitman's vision of America makes him its greatest poet.

---

[1] **stately:** graceful
[2] **near to me:** important to me
[3] **rhyme:** to create sentences or phrases that end in matching sounds: *He gave a* shout! *"The sun is* out!"
[4] **wealthy:** rich

13 SHARE WHAT YOU LEARNED

A. Work with a partner who read the same text.

1. Read the focus questions for your text.

2. Discuss the questions and write your answers.

Focus Questions for Text A

1. When and where was Cora Stewart born?

2. What did Cora Stewart learn from her job? How did that affect her?

3. How did Cora Stewart contribute to American society?

Focus Questions for Text B

1. When and where was Walt Whitman born?

2. What jobs did Walt Whitman have in his youth? How did they affect him?

3. How did Walt Whitman contribute to American society?

B. With your partner, find a pair who read a different text and form a team.

1. Share the topic of your text with your teammates.

2. Take turns sharing your answers to the focus questions.

3. Add any other information from the text that you remember.

14 SHARE WHAT YOU THINK

Discuss these questions with your teammates. Then share your answers with the class.

1. Compare Cora Stewart and Walt Whitman. How are they similar? How are they different?

2. Why do you think Walt Whitman is very famous in American history, but Cora Stewart is not?

3. Would you want Cora Stewart or Walt Whitman as a teacher? Why or why not?

4. Which of the following contributions do you think are most valuable to society? Explain your answers.

____ agricultural inventions   ____ philosophies

____ economic theories   ____ poetry

____ legal decisions   ____ scientific discoveries

____ musical compositions   ____ stories

15 REFLECT ON WHAT YOU READ IN THIS UNIT

Interview

Read the questions and think about your answers. Then work in small groups to interview each other. Decide on one person from history that you would all like to meet.

1. If you could meet anyone from history, who would you choose? Why?

2. Who do you think is an important individual living in the world today? Why? What makes this person unique?

Chart

Use the information in the chart to discuss the questions below with your classmates:

How College Students Learn New Material				
Lecture	Seminar	Lab Work	Field Work	Other
(Students listen to the instructor present the new material.)	(The instructor and students discuss the new material.)	(Students learn and work with new material in the laboratory.)	(Students learn new material in the real world.)	
82.7%	14.7%	21.8%	5.3%	7.4%

Based on a 1998 National Center for Educational Statistics survey of post-secondary instructors

- What can you infer from the chart about the teaching method professors most prefer?

- Predict how the percentages will change in the year 2020. Explain the reasons for your predictions.

Write

A. Work in small groups. Brainstorm a list of the world's problems.

B. Imagine that you are now famous for solving one of the world's problems. Write a short autobiography (a biography of yourself) that answers some or all of these questions:

- When and where were you born? What kind of childhood did you have?

- What did you study in school? What kind of jobs did you have?

- What world problem did you solve? How did you solve it?

Unit 7

Learning to Learn

In this unit you will:

● read about education in the U.S.
● learn how to find the main idea and supporting details in a paragraph

WHAT ARE YOUR IDEAS ABOUT EDUCATION?

A. Work in a small group. Look at the pictures and write sentences that compare the two classrooms. Explain which classroom you prefer and why.

B. Think about each statement and tell your classmates why you agree or disagree. Give examples to support your opinion.

1. To succeed in the workplace, you must succeed in school.

2. College is not for everybody.

3. There are many different ways to learn a subject.

A. **Ask and answer these questions about the chart with your classmates.**

- Where can you . . . ?
- How long do people study at a . . . ?

CONTINUING YOUR EDUCATION AFTER HIGH SCHOOL		
Institution	**You can . . .**	**Length of Time**
vocational school	**learn specific occupations** (office careers, technology, cosmetology, etc.)	1 month–2 years
military academy	**get training for the Army, Navy, Marines, or Air Force**	4 years
community college/ junior college	**get a degree in the Arts** (literature, music, history, drama, psychology, etc.)	2 years
college or university	**get a degree in the Sciences** (engineering, technology, chemistry, medicine, etc.) **get a degree in Business** (administration, operations, information technology)	4–8 years

B. **Guess which word or phrase has a meaning similar to the underlined word. Check your guesses after you read the article on pages 88–89.**

1. After they <u>graduate from</u> high school, students can continue their education in many ways.

    a. complete   b. begin   c. close

2. Because students' needs are <u>diverse</u>, there are various types of schools and training to choose from.

    a. few   b. difficult   c. different

3. Students who <u>attend</u> vocational schools get job training in areas such as baking, auto mechanics, and computer repair.

    a. wait for   b. go to   c. work for

4. Some students go to two-year community colleges and others go to colleges or universities that are four-year <u>institutions</u>.

    a. schools   b. buildings   c. classrooms

5. Students at state colleges usually pay lower <u>tuition</u> than students at private colleges.

    a. fees   b. wages   c. fines

> The **main ideas** in a text are the ideas the author thinks are the most important. Often, but not always, the main idea of a paragraph is in the first sentence. The other sentences in the paragraph have **supporting details** (facts or ideas) that give more information about the main idea.

Practice Finding the Main Idea and Supporting Ideas

Read this paragraph. It is from the next article you will read. Then answer the questions below with a partner.

A Look at Diversity in Higher Education

The men and women who attend U.S. colleges and universities come from diverse backgrounds. The current college population includes students from a wide range of ethnicities and from all income levels: low, middle, and high.

1. What is the main idea of the paragraph?

    a. Men and women go to U.S. colleges and universities.
    b. All kinds of people go to U.S. colleges and universities.
    c. There are three income levels: low, middle, and high.

2. Which of the following information supports the main idea.

    a. The current college population includes students.
    b. The current college population includes many ethnic groups.
    c. The current college population only includes students from high income levels.

Use Your Reading Skills

A. Preview the article on pages 88–89. Discuss these questions with your classmates.

    1. What is the topic of the article?

    2. What do you already know about this topic?

B. With a partner, predict what you will learn about the subjects below. Then check your predictions as you read the article on pages 88–89.

    a. early American colleges

    b. education for women

This article from an education journal discusses changes in university and college student populations in the U.S. over the last 250 years.

A Look at Diversity in Higher Education

The men and women who attend U.S. colleges and universities come from diverse backgrounds. The current college population includes students from a wide range of ethnicities and from all income levels: low, middle, and high.

5   Diversity[1] wasn't always part of American college life. When Harvard College in Massachusetts opened its doors in 1636, its first students were wealthy, white, and male. For the next 200 years, this was the typical college population. Many people simply didn't believe that women or minorities needed a college education. Fortunately,

10   not everyone shared that view. Students who were neither white nor male were able to go to separate and highly respected colleges such as Radcliffe for women and Howard University for African Americans.

    The U.S. government provided greater educational opportunities for Americans in 1944, with the GI Bill of Rights. In this bill, the

15   government promised to pay tuition and living costs for any World War II veteran[2] who wanted to go to college. The bill opened up U.S. campuses to students of all ethnic and economic backgrounds. As a result 2.5 million veterans attended college, and many of them graduated and became engineers, lawyers, and teachers.

20   Change happened slowly, however. Although the integration[3] of most colleges started with the GI Bill, campuses didn't have many minority students until the 1980s. Also, for a long time many parents didn't believe in the value of a college education for their daughters. Throughout the 20th century, Americans had to fight for equal rights

25   for all members of society. Thanks to their fight, the numbers of minorities and women in college increased over time.

    The number and diversity of college students continues to grow. In 1970, college enrollment was at 7.4 million; in 2001, it was more

[1] **diversity:** a large variety of people or things
[2] **veteran:** a person who was in the military but isn't now (an ex-soldier)
[3] **integration:** the end of a system of separating people of different races in a place

than 15 million. Now at least half of the students in U.S. colleges are
30 women and almost a third are minority students.

The United States doesn't have a national university system, but
it does have a national mindset[4] about higher education: *Education
equals opportunity.* These days, thanks to 250 years of changes, all
Americans have the right to get the education they need in order to
35 get the most out of the opportunities that come their way.

[4] **mindset:** a way of thinking

4 PROCESS WHAT YOU READ

A. **Discuss these questions with a partner. Scan the article to check your answers.**

1. In what ways are today's college and university students diverse?

2. Who was allowed to attend the first U.S. university?

3. What colleges could women and minorities attend when they were not able to go to all-male or all-white colleges?

4. What did the GI Bill promise to do?

5. What happened to the number of college students between 1970 and 2001?

6. Why do Americans believe education is important?

B. **Correct the statements so that each one expresses a main idea from the article. Look back at the article to check your answers.**

1. These days, U.S. college and university students come from ~~similar~~ *diverse* backgrounds.

2. The first American college students were wealthy white women.

3. The 1944 GI Bill helped veterans go to high school.

4. Changes in American higher education happened quickly.

5. College enrollment is decreasing.

6. Americans believe that education equals diversity.

C. **Discuss these questions in small groups. Share your answers with the class.**

1. What are the benefits of going to school with people from different backgrounds?

2. What are the benefits of going to school with people from the same background?

5 WORK WITH THE VOCABULARY

A. Fill in the missing adjective forms of the nouns in the chart. Scan the article to find them. Hint: Look for words that begin with the first few letters of the noun.

	Noun	Paragraph	Adjective
a.	diversity	1	diverse
b.	wealth	2	
c.	ethnicity	3	
d.	equality	4	
e.	nation	6	

B. Use the nouns and adjectives from the chart to complete the paragraph below.

College classes are no longer filled with _____ *white men.*
Women and men from _____ *economic and*
_____ *backgrounds sit in college classes around the U.S.*
Thanks to this _____ *, college class discussions provide a*
_____ *of viewpoints and ideas!*

C. Read these sentences about social changes in the U.S. Choose the correct noun or adjective form to complete each sentence.

1. The population of 21st century America is (diverse/diversity).

2. One of the benefits of this (diversity/diverse) is the great variety of cultures and ideas in U.S. education, government, and business.

3. In the past, however, most (nation/national) decisions were made by (wealth/wealthy) white men.

4. (Wealth/Wealthy) played an important role in American society.

5. At that time, there was no (equality/equal) for minorities or women.

6. A person's (ethnicity/ethnic) often decided his or her future.

7. It was a difficult time for the (nation/national).

8. After many years, minorities and women won the fight for (equality/equal) rights for all people, no matter what their religion, gender, economic or (ethnicity/ethnic) background is.

A. Discuss the statements about college life in small groups and explain why you agree or disagree. Give examples to support your opinion.

1. Football players are the most popular people on a college campus.
   I agree. Football players are always in the school newspaper.
   I disagree. Many different types of people are popular.

2. Wealthy people don't have to study hard.

3. Smart female students don't have boyfriends.

4. College students go to parties all weekend long.

B. Guess which words have a meaning similar to the underlined words. Check your guesses after you read the article on page 92.

1. It's <u>a myth</u> that college life is one big party. Classes and homework can be very difficult.
   - a. true
   - b. not true
   - c. interesting

2. College life is <u>frequently</u> the subject of American movies. There's at least one new movie about college students every year.
   - a. rarely
   - b. sometimes
   - c. often

3. Writing for the school newspaper, volunteering, and playing sports are some <u>extracurricular</u> activities that college students enjoy.
   - a. additional
   - b. expensive
   - c. romantic

4. Most American college students today come from families with <u>moderate</u> incomes.
   - a. low
   - b. high
   - c. average

Use Your Reading Skills

Preview the first and last paragraph of the article on page 92. Predict which ideas below will *not* be in this article and mark them with a check (✓).

_____ 1. American movies about college life are entertaining.

_____ 2. Hollywood makes movies that show stories of real college life.

_____ 3. To learn about a college, read its brochure or website, or visit the campus.

_____ 4. There is nothing exciting happening on America's college campuses.

College life is frequently a subject of American movies, but much of what we see on the screen isn't reality, it's entertainment. The following information is from the American Colleges and Universities website.

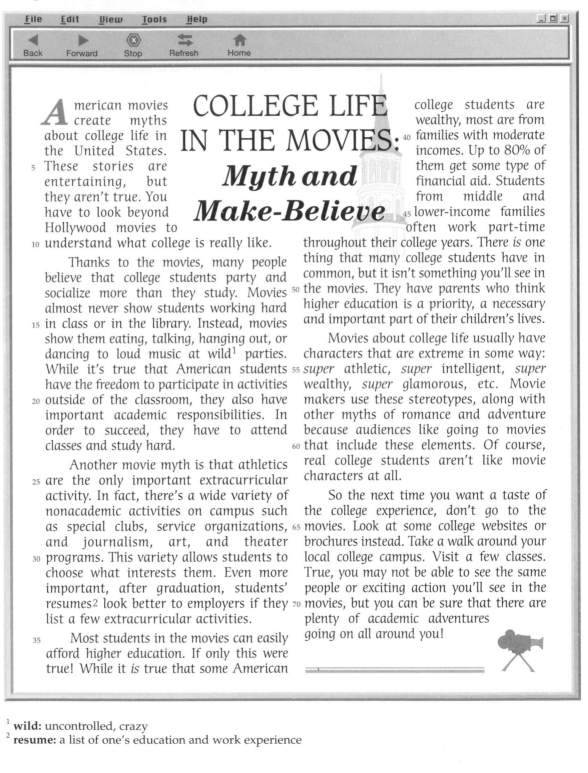

File   Edit   View   Tools   Help

Back   Forward   Stop   Refresh   Home

COLLEGE LIFE IN THE MOVIES:
Myth and Make-Believe

American movies create myths about college life in the United States.
5 These stories are entertaining, but they aren't true. You have to look beyond Hollywood movies to
10 understand what college is really like.

Thanks to the movies, many people believe that college students party and socialize more than they study. Movies almost never show students working hard
15 in class or in the library. Instead, movies show them eating, talking, hanging out, or dancing to loud music at wild[1] parties. While it's true that American students have the freedom to participate in activities
20 outside of the classroom, they also have important academic responsibilities. In order to succeed, they have to attend classes and study hard.

Another movie myth is that athletics
25 are the only important extracurricular activity. In fact, there's a wide variety of nonacademic activities on campus such as special clubs, service organizations, and journalism, art, and theater
30 programs. This variety allows students to choose what interests them. Even more important, after graduation, students' resumes[2] look better to employers if they list a few extracurricular activities.

35 Most students in the movies can easily afford higher education. If only this were true! While it *is* true that some American college students are wealthy, most are from
40 families with moderate incomes. Up to 80% of them get some type of financial aid. Students from middle and
45 lower-income families often work part-time throughout their college years. There *is* one thing that many college students have in common, but it isn't something you'll see in
50 the movies. They have parents who think higher education is a priority, a necessary and important part of their children's lives.

Movies about college life usually have characters that are extreme in some way:
55 *super* athletic, *super* intelligent, *super* wealthy, *super* glamorous, etc. Movie makers use these stereotypes, along with other myths of romance and adventure because audiences like going to movies
60 that include these elements. Of course, real college students aren't like movie characters at all.

So the next time you want a taste of the college experience, don't go to the
65 movies. Look at some college websites or brochures instead. Take a walk around your local college campus. Visit a few classes. True, you may not be able to see the same people or exciting action you'll see in the
70 movies, but you can be sure that there are plenty of academic adventures going on all around you!

---

[1] **wild:** uncontrolled, crazy
[2] **resume:** a list of one's education and work experience

8 PROCESS WHAT YOU READ

Identify the main idea for each paragraph. Compare answers with a partner.

Paragraph 1

   a. Movies about college life are fun to watch.
   b. You should look beyond college movies to understand college life.
   c. Colleges in the movies are not like real colleges.

Paragraph 2

   a. Movies almost never show students in the library or in class.
   b. Movies show college students partying more than studying, but American students study hard.
   c. American students have to attend classes and study hard to succeed.

Paragraph 3

   a. In the movies, sports is the only extracurricular activity on campus.
   b. There are many extracurricular activities on campus.
   c. Participating in extra curricular activities can help students get a job later.

Paragraph 4

   a. Most college students' families are not wealthy.
   b. Most students work part-time in college.
   c. Most college students in movies get financial aid.

Paragraph 5

   a. Audiences like movies that present extreme characters.
   b. Movie-makers usually show college students who are extreme.
   c. College students are rarely super athletic or super intelligent.

9 WORK WITH THE VOCABULARY

Scan the article to find each of the words below. Then underline the nearby word or phrase in the text that has a similar meaning.

1. myth   (Paragraph 1)   _____*stories*_____

2. party (*v.*)   (Paragraph 2)   _____

3. extracurricular activity   (Paragraph 3)   _____

4. priority   (Paragraph 4)   _____

A. Imagine that you can't cook, but you want to learn. Rank the ways you would choose to learn (1–3). Compare answers with your classmates.

_____ **a.** have an experienced cook tell you what to do

_____ **b.** buy some different ingredients and experiment

_____ **c.** read a recipe with pictures

B. Imagine that you have to do a class project about the main ideas in a story you have read. Circle the project you would most like to do. Underline the project you would least like to do.

a. draw pictures or take photos   **d.** make a timeline

b. write a report   **e.** create a dance

c. lead a discussion   **f.** write a song

Compare choices with your classmates. Which project was the most popular? the least popular?

C. Preview the texts starting on page 94 and on page 96. Then answer these questions.

1. What is the topic of text A?

2. What is the topic of text B?

D. Choose one text to read. Then answer these questions.

1. What is the title of the text?

2. What do you already know about this topic?

3. What do you predict you will learn more about?

11 **READ A**

Educators know that not everyone has the same way of learning new information. Different people have different learning styles—they prefer different ways of "taking in" information. This excerpt from a textbook discusses three types of learning styles.

Learning About Learning: Learning Styles

People learn in different ways. Some students want their teachers to write everything on the board. Others prefer to listen. Some take notes, some doodle or draw in their notebooks. Others like to discuss questions in small groups. Educational researchers[1] studied student behavior to find out how different people learn. Researchers give different names to different learning styles, but they all agree that students who understand their own styles can improve their study skills. The learning styles described below (visual, auditory, and tactile) are just three of the many ways to identify how people learn.

Visual learners have to "see it to believe it." They often have good imaginations (they can picture things in their minds), and they may also have a good sense of color and artistic ability. These learners may have trouble listening to lectures or instructions if there are no pictures or text to support what they hear. They may also find it hard to focus in a room where people are moving around. If you are a visual learner, you can use charts and graphs to help you study. You can also try drawing pictures or symbols in your notes to help you remember ideas. Some visual learners like to use colorful pens or highlighters to focus on important ideas in their reading.

Auditory learners remember information if they hear it. They prefer to learn by listening and will often ask questions about things they read. Reading assignments can be difficult for these learners, and they can quickly lose their focus if there is too much noise in a room. Auditory learners can improve their study skills by working in study groups where they can quiz each other. If you are an auditory learner with a reading assignment, tape yourself reading or summarizing the text aloud. Then you can study by playing back the tape.

Tactile learners can learn and remember what they touch. That's why computers are a big help to these learners; the sense of touch (using the keyboard) helps them remember information. Tactile learners prefer to do "hands-on" activities such as role plays, science experiments, or projects they can build. They learn better when they do some sort of physical activity. Tactile learners need to take frequent breaks when they study because they don't like sitting for long periods of time. If you are a tactile learner with a lot of studying to do, try taking a walk or exercising while you memorize information.

Many schools use questionnaires to help students identify the ways they learn best. Often teachers take classes to learn techniques that match different learning styles. One thing is true for all learners, whether visual, auditory, or tactile—in the world of education, one of the most important subjects is learning how to learn.

---

[1] **researcher:** someone who studies something carefully and reports what he or she finds out

Dr. Howard Gardner is famous for his theory of Multiple Intelligences, which identifies the different ways that people are "smart." This article from an academic journal gives an overview of the theory.

LEARNING ABOUT LEARNING:
Multiple Intelligences

For more than 200 years, in the traditional American classroom, a teacher stood at the front of the class and lectured on a topic. Students sat in their chairs, listening and taking notes. For homework students read their textbooks. They memorized information and took tests to show what they learned.
5 Traditional education taught people to believe that being intelligent meant remembering information and writing about it. Society thought that people without strong language or mathematical skills were less intelligent, even if they had other abilities such as drawing, building, or working with animals.

Toward the end of the 20th century, researchers learned that different parts
10 of the brain control different abilities such as the ability to use language, make music, or move. One area of the brain may be stronger than another. For example, the part of the brain that controls musical ability may be stronger than the one that controls language use.

Dr. Howard Gardner, a Harvard professor, used brain research to develop
15 his theory of Multiple Intelligences (MI). For example, Gardner knew that people can have a great deal of musical ability, even though they can't read or write well. He believed that musical ability was just one type of intelligence, and that reading or writing well were other types. Gardner wanted to identify the different intelligences that people have. He asked himself, "What are the things
20 that people do in the world? . . . What abilities do you need to do those things?" By answering those questions, he identified eight types of intelligences:

People who are good at . . .	usually have this intelligence.
playing or understanding music	musical
dancing or playing sports	bodily / kinesthetic
25 solving mathematical problems	math / logical
using language	verbal
drawing or designing	spatial
working with other people	interpersonal
working by themselves	intrapersonal
30 identifying patterns in nature	naturalist

The idea that there are at least eight ways to be "smart" is causing changes in American education. Teachers are more likely to provide students with interpersonal tasks or kinesthetic projects. Many tests allow students to demonstrate their intelligence in a variety of ways, such as interpreting a drawing, writing a paragraph, or analyzing a chart. Thanks to brain research and Howard Gardner, attitudes towards nontraditional teaching approaches are changing, and so is the American classroom.

❖

13 SHARE WHAT YOU LEARNED

A. Work with a partner who read the same text.

1. Read the focus questions for your text.

2. Discuss the questions and write your answers.

Focus Questions for Text A

1. What are the main ideas in this article?

2. How did researchers discover learning styles?

3. Name and describe three learning styles.

Focus Questions for Text B

1. What are the main ideas in this article?

2. What questions helped Howard Gardner identify the intelligences?

3. Name three types of intelligences and explain them.

B. With your partner, find a pair who read a different text and form a team.

1. Share the topic of your text with your teammates.

2. Take turns sharing your answers to the focus questions.

3. Add any other information from the text that you remember.

14 SHARE WHAT YOU THINK

Discuss these questions with your teammates. Then share your answers with the class.

1. Is it a good idea for teachers to identify their students' learning styles?

2. Which intelligences and/or learning styles do you think are most common?

3. Which learning styles or intelligences are important in countries other than the U.S.?

4. If you could improve one of your intelligences, which one would it be? Why?

15 REFLECT ON WHAT YOU READ IN THIS UNIT

Interview

Read the questions and think about your answers. Then interview a partner. With your partner, decide on a class you would both like to take.

1. What are your educational plans for the future?

2. How does this class fit into those plans?

3. If you could take a class in any subject, what subject would you choose? Why?

4. What advice do you have for students who want to succeed?

Chart

A. Survey ten classmates using the questions below. Use tick marks (卌) to record *yes* or *no* answers.

Do you . . .	Yes	No
know people from more than one ethnic group?		
have a friend from an ethnic group that is different from yours?		
know people from economic backgrounds that are different from yours?		
have a friend from a different economic background?		

B. Discuss these questions with your classmates.

1. Did anything in your survey surprise you?

2. Based on the results of the survey, do you think diversity is part of students' daily lives?

Write

A. Work with a partner. Silently guess each other's strongest learning style and intelligence. Share your guesses and the clues you used to make them. Say whether your partner's guesses were correct.

B. Write a paragraph about your learning style and intelligences. Answer some or all of these questions:

*   What type of learner are you?

*   What is your strongest intelligence? your weakest intelligence?

*   How do your intelligences affect your life?

*   Do you think learning about learning is important? Why or why not?

Unit 8

Play Time

In this unit you will:

● read about attitudes toward time in the U.S.
● learn how to summarize what you read

HOW DO YOU FEEL ABOUT TIME?

A. Look at the cartoon and discuss it with your classmates. Where are these people? How do they feel? How do you feel when you wait in line?

B. Read each statement and decide if it is true or false. Compare responses with your classmates.

Statement	True	False
1. I usually have to do several things at once.		
2. I don't like it when people are late.		
3. I rarely wear a watch.		
4. I often watch the clock during class.		
5. I never have enough time to do everything I need to do.		
6. I have a lot of time to visit with my friends.		

A. Imagine that you have a three-week vacation that starts tomorrow. In a small group share your answers to these questions:

  1. Will you stay at home or travel? Why?

  2. What types of things will you forget about?

  3. Which friends will you see?

  4. What types of things will you do every day?

B. Work with a partner. Guess which word or phrase has a meaning similar to the underlined word or phrase. Check your guesses after you read the article on pages 102–103.

  1. Arlene is a writer. When she gets too stressed out, she needs to <u>take time off</u>.

      a. take an airplane   b. take a break

  2. Camping is one of Arlene's favorite <u>leisure activity</u>. She also enjoys swimming.

      a. things to eat   b. things to do

  3. When Arlene and her family <u>go camping</u>, they borrow their neighbors' tent.

      a. sleep outdoors   b. work indoors

  4. Arlene is always surprised by her family's <u>laziness</u> on these trips. They don't want to help her cook or clean up after meals. They just want to sit and look at the lake.

      a. not wanting to eat   b. not wanting to work

  5. Sometimes Arlene <u>feels guilty</u> that she's on vacation when other people are hard at work. The feeling only lasts for a minute though.

      a. feels bad   b. feels angry

  6. After a vacation, Arlene <u>increases her productivity</u>. She's so relaxed that she can write 10 to 20 pages in one day.

      a. is able to produce a little   b. is able to produce a lot

C. Discuss these questions with your partner.

  1. Do you ever take time off? When?

  2. What are your favorite pastimes?

  3. Do you like to go camping?

  4. Is laziness always bad? Why or why not?

  5. Do you feel guilty when you take a break from studying? Why or why not?

  6. Does a study break increase or decrease your productivity? Why?

> **Summarizing** a text means using your own words to create a short version of the most important information in the text. A summary includes information that answers questions such as *Who? What? Where? What happened? When? How?* and *Why?* Summarizing helps you remember important information and allows you to share it with other people.

Practice Summarizing

A. Read the paragraph and underline the most important information. Compare answers with your classmates.

Not More Free Time—Less Busy Time

by E. Rose

Many people say they need more free time, but maybe that's not true. Maybe what <u>people need</u> is <u>less "busy" time</u>. Many people in the U.S. are trying to do too many things at one time. For example, a salesperson isn't just helping a customer; she's also talking on the phone to her manager and hanging up clothes on a rack. A customer isn't just buying a blouse; she's talking on her cell phone and looking after her children. The problem with multitasking (working on many things at once) is that it's hard to do something well when you're not focusing on it. Also, multitasking can be very tiring. If you want to feel more relaxed, do one thing at a time. For example, the next time someone phones you while you're doing something else, say you'll call back, when you're not so busy.

B. Write a summary of the paragraph by answering these questions in your own words. Compare summaries with a partner.

1. What does the author think that people need? Why?

2. Why is multitasking a problem?

3. What does the author tell people to do to feel more relaxed?

Use Your Reading Skills

Preview the comprehension questions in exercise A on page 103. Highlight the answers as you read the article.

Vacationing is a common American pastime, but many people are uncomfortable taking time off. This book review tells the history of Americans' mixed feelings about vacations.

A Look at the History of American Vacations

WORKING AT PLAY
By Cindy S. Aron

Before the 1850s, Americans never went on vacation. In fact, there was no word *vacation* in their vocabulary. Even today,
5 taking time off from work makes many Americans uncomfortable. In her book *Working at Play*, Professor Cindy S. Aron tells the story of Americans' love-hate
10 relationship with vacations.

Aron shows how early American history can explain these mixed feelings about vacations. When the Puritans[1] emigrated[2] from England
15 to the American colonies in the 1600s, they brought with them a strong belief in productivity and an equally strong disapproval of laziness. Aron points out that these
20 Puritan values don't support the idea of "getting away from it all" or going on vacation.

Vacationing started in the 1850s. At that time, wealthy people left the
25 cities and lived in their country homes for the summer. These people never spoke of this as a vacation, though. Instead, they said they were "going away for their

30 health." Aron explains that deadly contagious diseases,[3] such as cholera and tuberculosis, spread quickly in the hot, crowded cities, so going away was a healthy thing to do. Later,
35 doctors said that traveling and camping were also good for a person's health, so wealthy people began to do these activities as well.

Working-class Americans began
40 to take vacations in the middle of the 20th century. By the 1950s, most workers had time off with pay. The average American family didn't have a home in the country, but they
45 could go camping in a national park or stay in an inexpensive motel. Taking a vacation became a part of the American way of life.

Even though modern-day society
50 accepts the idea of vacations, Aron points out that Puritan values continue to affect the kinds of vacations Americans take. For some people, vacation time has to be
55 productive, or they feel guilty. During their time off, these vacationers often choose to help the environment or build schools and housing in poor communities. Some people find it
60 impossible to leave their work behind when they go on a vacation. Aron explains that thanks to technology

---

[1] **Puritans:** a group of people who came to the colonies for religious freedom.
[2] **emigrate:** to move from one country to another
[3] **contagious disease:** an illness that moves from person to person through the air or through contact

(beepers, cell phones, and laptop computers), these vacationers have
65 the opportunity to create portable offices anywhere they go.

In her book, Aron doesn't suggest that people should change their attitudes towards leisure time.
70 Instead, she lets history explain what by now is clear: most Americans like to add work to their play.

Adapted from a review of *Working at Play: A History of Vacations in the United States* by Cindy S. Aron

4 PROCESS WHAT YOU READ

A. Write the answers to these questions in your own words. Look back at the book review to check your answers.

1. What reason does the author give for Americans' mixed feelings about vacations?

2. Who were the first American vacationers? Where did they go?

3. What does Aron point out about these first vacations?

4. When did working-class Americans start vacationing? What did they do?

5. How do Puritan values continue to affect how Americans take vacations?

6. What does history show about Americans' attitudes toward leisure time?

B. Write a brief summary of the book review. Use your answers to questions 1–6 above to help you. Compare summaries with a partner.

C. Choose the best heading for paragraphs 2–5 of the book review. Discuss your choices with your classmates.

Paragraph 2

    a. The Strength of Puritan Values

    b. Lazy People Don't Need Vacations

    c. Puritans Have Mixed Feelings

Paragraph 3

    a. Buying a House in the Country

    b. Getting Away for Their Health

    c. Spreading Deadly Diseases

Paragraph 4

    a. Vacations for Under $100

    b. Camping in the 1960s

    c. The Average American Goes on Vacation

Paragraph 5

    a. The Guilty Vacation

    b. The Productive Vacation

    c. The Portable Vacation

A. Match the words and phrases on the left with their definitions. Look back at the book review on pages 102–103 to check your answers.

_____ **1.** get away from it all   a. free time

_____ **2.** disapproval   b. able to go anywhere

_____ **3.** portable   c. contagious disease of the lungs

_____ **4.** tuberculosis   d. unfavorable opinion

_____ **5.** leisure time   e. take a vacation

B. Use these words to complete Mariko's letter to her co-workers.

a. get away from

b. guilty

c. mixed feelings

d. opportunity

e. time off

f. productive

Hi Everyone,

I'm writing to you from sunny Cairo. Egypt is beautiful and I'm having a wonderful time. I have __c__ about telling you this, because I know you're busy
                    1
at work and I'm not there to help you, but I'm working hard here too. I'm so happy that I can use my ___ to help the people in a nearby village build a
                                     2
new school.

We start work early in the morning, but at lunchtime we stop for several hours. No one feels ___ about this because it's absolutely necessary in the
                      3
summertime heat. Even if we tried to work, we wouldn't be ___.
                                                          4

Last weekend I went to the museum in Cairo. It was very interesting and a great way to ___ the heat! This is a fascinating country and I hope some of
                5
you will have the ___ to travel here soon.
                  6

See you in a few weeks.

Best,

Mariko

GET READY TO READ ABOUT: Space Vacations

A. Look at the cartoon and answer the questions with your classmates.

Your turn to get it.

1. Where are the astronauts? What are they playing? What's the problem?

2. Do you think people will vacation in space in the future? Why or why not?

3. Imagine that you're going on a space vacation. You will have all the food and clothing you need. You can take three of these recreational items with you. Which ones will you choose? Mark your choices with a check (✓).

____ ball ____ binoculars ____ books

____ CDs and CD player ____ deck of cards ____ musical instrument

____ video games ____ other _____

B. Put a check (✓) next to the words you know. Ask your classmates for the definitions of the words you don't know. Look up the words no one knows in a dictionary.

____ concentrate ____ expensive ____ science fiction

____ space station ____ stars ____ tourist

Use Your Reading Skills

Preview the article on page 106 and the statements at the top of page 107. Then guess whether the statements are true or false. Check your guesses as you read.

Recreation is an important part of every astronaut's day, but if some businesspeople have their way, astronauts won't be the only ones playing in space. This magazine article looks at recreation in space, both present and future.

SPACE: THE VACATION OF THE FUTURE?

When you watch videos of astronauts, floating[1] from place to place in their spaceship, it's easy to believe that an astronaut's life is a restful vacation among the stars. In reality, however, astronauts don't have free time. Because space missions are very short and expensive, NASA[2] plans
5 every minute of the astronauts' days so that they can perform hundreds of routine[3] tasks and complete many complicated, difficult assignments. That is not to say that astronauts work all the time. Play is an important part of their day, too. Along with specific times to sleep, eat, wash up, work, and exercise, they also have time to play on their daily schedules.

10 Astronauts are under a lot of stress. They have to work in a small space with several people, do the same tasks perfectly, day after day, and manage the uncomfortable body changes that happen in space.

NASA psychologists know that in order for astronauts to do their best work, they must be able to concentrate. Recreational, or fun, activities help
15 people focus, do their tasks well, and feel less stressed. NASA gives astronauts special recreation kits that include different types of balls, music CDs, a CD player, books, a deck of cards, and binoculars for looking at Earth. These items give astronauts a mental vacation from their very difficult work.

20 Science fiction films show astronauts and their passengers stopping at space stations for R&R (rest and recreation). At this time, there's no room or time for tourists on the space shuttle. However, Gene Myers, president of the Space Island Group, believes that a space hotel is not science fiction. He's planning a commercial space
25 station that will be a place to work and vacation by 2010. Myers is not alone. NASA is working with other countries to build an international space station. Hilton hotels and Bigelow Aerospace and Space Adventures are also planning their own space hotels. Many people believe that space tourism will be one of the most
30 successful businesses in the 21st century.

So, the next time you watch astronauts float across your television screen, think about making a reservation for a space vacation. Just don't forget to take your recreation kit along; it's a long trip to the hotel!

Information adapted from Space Science Group at Northwestern State University

[2] **float:** to move slowly and lightly through the air
[2] **NASA:** National Aeronautics and Space Administration, the agency in charge of the U.S. space program
[3] **routine:** regular, usual

8 PROCESS WHAT YOU READ

A. Read each statement and decide if it's true (*T*) or false (*F*).

_F_ **1.** There's a lot of time to complete work on a space mission.

____ **2.** NASA plans every minute of an astronaut's day.

____ **3.** Life in the space shuttle can be stressful and uncomfortable.

____ **4.** Recreation helps astronauts concentrate on their work.

____ **5.** NASA is working with other countries to build a space station.

____ **6.** No one believes that people will vacation in space someday.

B. Read the summary of the article "Space: The Vacation of the Future?" Each sentence is incorrect. Cross out the word that makes each sentence incorrect and replace it with a correct word. Then look back at the article to check your answers.

Because astronauts have so much work to do, and their work is very ~~relaxing,~~ _stressful_

NASA schedules weekly recreation times to increase stress and reduce concentration.

Astronauts use satellite repair kits to relax and have fun. The author points out that

even though people aren't currently vacationing in space, space tourism will be

successful in the 20th century. Gene Myers of the Space Island Group is raising money

to buy a commercial space station because he thinks that people will want to go on

vacation there by 2020.

9 WORK WITH THE VOCABULARY

Match the words in the left column with the words in the right column that have similar meanings. Look back at the article to check your answers.

____ **1.** concentrate   a. travel business

____ **2.** complicated   b. job

____ **3.** perform   c. stories about the future

____ **4.** recreational   d. plan

____ **5.** science fiction   e. focus

____ **6.** task   f. fun

____ **7.** schedule   g. difficult

____ **8.** tourism industry   h. do

A. Look at the cartoon and describe what is happening in the picture. Do you think it is funny? Why or why not? Discuss your answers with your classmates.

WELL-EARNED VACATION

B. Read these common expressions about time. What do the expressions tell you about American attitudes toward time? Discuss your ideas with your classmates.

- give time

- make good use of time

- never enough time

- spend time

- use time wisely

- waste time

C. Preview the texts on pages 109 and 110 and answer these questions.

1. What are these texts about?

2. What do you know about these topics?

D. Choose one text to read. Then answer these questions.

1. What is the title of the text?

2. What is the topic of the text?

3. What do you already know about this topic?

4. Do you predict that you will find the topic interesting? Why? Why not?

How do Americans manage their mixed feelings about vacations? For some, a volunteer vacation is the answer. This web page discusses this popular way to spend leisure time.

File   Edit   View   Tools   Help

◄ Back   ► Forward   ⊗ Stop   ⇄ Refresh   ⌂ Home

GUILT-FREE *Vacations*

Volunteering is an American tradition. People in the U.S. volunteer for hundreds of different organizations. People of all ages do
5 community service projects with children, the homeless, the elderly, and the disabled. Even though they receive no pay for their time, volunteers know that their work
10 makes a difference in the world.

A recent poll found that over one-third of Americans currently volunteer or volunteered at one time in their lives. What the poll doesn't
15 mention is the growing number of people who use vacation time to volunteer. These days, volunteers all over the country use their vacations to help preserve[1] and protect America's
20 environment, culture, and history. The vacation projects vary: from working in the national parks, to whale or butterfly counting, to collecting and labeling artifacts.[2]

25 **Some vacation volunteers spend a week or two in the national parks or forests, building and repairing hundreds of miles of trails, or paths.** Typically, vacationers work six to eight
30 hours and share camp chores, including cooking, washing dishes, and collecting firewood. These trips cost about the same as a two-night stay in an inexpensive motel.

35 **Vacation volunteers who want a different experience can contribute to U.S. cultural history.** One project works to preserve New Mexico's ancient cliff dwellings (the 3,000-year-
40 old homes of Native Americans). Volunteers work long days and usually camp near the work site. They have to pay for their transportation to New Mexico, but not for their food.

45 **While this type of vacation may sound ideal, Bill McMillion, author of *Volunteer Vacations: Short-Term Adventures That Will Benefit You and Others*, tells people to choose their
50 vacations carefully.** He says volunteers should pick something they really want to do because once they start, they can't say, "Oh, today I'd rather do something else."

55 **A volunteer vacation is a great solution for Americans who believe that leisure isn't as important as being productive.** Volunteers know they will be physically active and use
60 their time wisely. Of course, they will also have opportunities to explore new places, meet new people, and have fun. For a culture that likes to add work to play, this is the perfect,
65 100% guilt-free vacation!

[1] **preserve:** to keep in good condition
[2] **artifact:** an object from the past

This essay is based on research from the Merk Family Fund survey and a Harris poll. It talks about how Americans are trying to make time to do what they feel is really important: spend time with friends and family.

Taking Time

Susan Ruiz

*B*ack in the 1960s, futurists[1] predicted that the biggest problem for Americans in the year 2000 would be managing all their free time. What happened? People in the U.S. have all the timesaving tools they could want: jet travel, cellular phones, microwave ovens, personal computers, faxes, VCRs. Yet they work more, not less.

5 Unstructured time—a day just to spend time with friends or family—is hard to find. Unfortunately, the futurists had it backwards. The more technology a society has, the less free time it has. Americans in most cities feel that time is scarce, that there's never enough of it.

According to social psychologist, Robert Levine, we're experiencing "a time
10 famine."[2] We're hungry for time. People use their cell phones to stay in touch with work when they're shopping for dinner or at the beach on the weekend. They have computers and fax machines at home so that they can be productive at any time of day or night. Everyone has 24 hours a day, of course. What Americans say they don't have is time to spend with people who are important to them. In a recent
15 survey, nearly three-quarters of the respondents said they needed more time with family and friends, and less stress, in order to feel satisfied.[3]

A recent Harris poll showed that American leisure time decreased almost 40 percent within the past 20 years, but that's only half the story. During that time, Americans' consumption (buying things) increased by 45 percent. When people
20 buy more, they have to work more so they can pay for the things they buy. One question on the poll asked if people agreed with the statement "Most of us buy and consume far more than we need." Eighty-two percent of the respondents said yes.

There is good news. Many people in the United States are trying to take back their time. Some people are choosing to have fewer possessions[4] and work less. Some
25 people are changing priorities and making time for family and friends. Others are turning off their cell phones and taking time for leisure activities: walking along a beach at sunset, hiking up a hill to see the sunrise, taking a child to the park for the afternoon. Americans are discovering that they want these things back, and they're the kinds of things that only time can buy.

[1] **futurist:** a person who thinks about the future
[2] **famine:** a terrible situation, when there isn't enough of something you need
[3] **satisfied:** content, happy
[4] **possession:** a thing you have such as a car, furniture, clothing, etc.

13 SHARE WHAT YOU LEARNED

A. Work with a partner who read the same text.

1. Read the focus questions for your text.

2. Discuss the questions and write your answers.

Focus Questions for Text A

1. What is volunteering and what role does it play in American life?

2. What is a volunteer vacation? Describe two types of volunteer vacations.

3. Why do Americans like volunteer vacations?

Focus Questions for Text B

1. What did futurists in the 1960s believe about the effect of technology?

2. What is a time famine? Why are Americans experiencing this famine?

3. What are some Americans doing to take back their time?

B. With your partner, find a pair who read a different text and form a team.

1. Share the topic of your text with your teammates.

2. Take turns sharing your answers to the focus questions.

3. Add any other information from the text that you remember.

14 SHARE WHAT YOU THINK

Discuss these questions with your teammates. Then share your answers with the class.

1. Do you think volunteer vacations are a good idea? Why or why not?

2. Is there a difference between the way you think about time and the usual way of thinking about time in the U.S.? Explain.

3. Is there a difference between the way you think about vacations and the usual way of thinking about vacations in the U.S.? Explain.

4. Imagine that a busy, stressed-out friend tells you he or she isn't enjoying life and asks for advice. What advice would you give?

15 REFLECT ON WHAT YOU READ IN THIS UNIT

Interview

Read the questions and think about your answers. Then interview a partner.
With your partner, find one activity that you both like to do.

1. When you aren't in school or studying, what other things do you do with
   your time?

2. Which of these activities do you think are productive? Which are not? Why?

   listening to CDs   playing sports

   spending time with friends   surfing the Internet

   taking trips   watching TV

Chart

A. Survey ten classmates, using the question below. Use tick marks (卌) to record
   their answers in the chart.

   How much free time do you have now compared with ten years ago?

FREE TIME		
Same	**More**	**Less**

B. Look at the results in your chart. Discuss them with your classmates.

Write

A. Read or reread the article on page 110. Work with a partner to summarize the
   ideas.

B. Write a paragraph that discusses your feelings about time and answers some
   or all of these questions:

   • Do you believe that there is a time famine? Why or why not?

   • Is it more important to spend time at work or with family and friends? Why?

   • What do you consider a waste of time?

   • How do you spend your time? What advice do you have for people who feel
     they don't have enough time?

Answer Key

Unit 1 Reaching Out

HOW DO YOU FEEL ABOUT MEETING NEW PEOPLE?

Exercise A (p. 1) (*Answers vary.*)

Exercise B (p. 1) (*Answers vary.*)

1. GET READY TO READ ABOUT: Social Anxiety

Exercise A (p. 2) (*Answers vary.*)

Exercise B (p. 2)
1. a   2. b   3. b   4. c

Exercise C (p. 2) (*Answers vary.*)

2. BUILDING READING SKILLS: Previewing 1

Practice Previewing (p. 3)
1. Making Friends
2. Bea Pal
3. *College News*
4. (*Answers vary.*)

Use Your Reading Skills (p. 3)
1. social anxiety and making new friends
2. college students
3. identifying social anxiety, getting help from counselors, and improving one's social life

4. PROCESS WHAT YOU READ

Exercise A (p. 5)
1. b   2. a   3. b   4. c

Exercise B (p. 5)
1. c   2. d or a   3. a   4. b

5. WORK WITH THE VOCABULARY

Exercise A (p. 6)
1. c   2. b   3. a   4. b   5. c   6. a

Exercise B (p. 6)
1. d   2. b   3. e   4. a   5. c

6. GET READY TO READ ABOUT: Shyness

Personality Quiz (p. 7)
1. a
2. b
3. someone who doesn't like large groups, but isn't shy.

7. BUILDING READING SKILLS: Previewing 2

Use Your Reading Skills (p. 7)
1. c   2. b   3. b

9. PROCESS WHAT YOU READ

Exercise A (p. 9)
4, 3, 6, 5, 2, 1

Exercise B (p. 9)
1. Male. He says, "I'm a shy guy."
2. College student. He says, "I think there are more students like me…"
3. Single. He says, "It's going to be a small wedding."

10. WORK WITH THE VOCABULARY (p. 9)

1. c   2. b   3. d   4. a   5. e

11. GET READY TO READ AND SHARE

Exercise A (p. 10) (*Answers vary.*)

Exercise B (p. 10) (*Answers vary.*)

Exercise C (p. 10)
1. The topic is body language and the pictures show different types of body language.
2. The topic is shaking hands and the pictures show different handshakes.

Exercise D (p. 10) (*Answers vary.*)

14. SHARE WHAT YOU LEARNED (p. 13)

Focus Questions for Text A
1. an expert on body language
2. your interest in what you see or hear
3. leaning forward – very interested; leaning back = not interested; arms and legs uncrossed, hands open = agree; arms and legs crossed, hands in fists = disagree; head to one side, eyes half open = thinking; foot tapping = tired of listening; slumped in a chair = bored; looking to the side while talking = maybe not telling the truth
4. see above

Focus Questions for Text B
1. a management consultant
2. you look into another person's eyes, grasp his or her whole hand, and pump it two or three times
3. an uncomfortable handshake pulls your fingers or twists and crushes your hand; a Palm Pinch uses only a few fingers; a Dead Fish slides out of your hand
4. because it's an important part of body language and to being successful

15. SHARE WHAT YOU THINK (p. 13) (*Answers vary.*)

16. REFLECT ON WHAT YOU READ IN THIS UNIT (p. 14) (*Answers vary.*)

Unit 2 A Need for Privacy

WHAT KINDS OF NEIGHBORS DO YOU HAVE?

Exercise A (p. 15) (*Answers vary.*)

Exercise B (p. 15) (*Answers vary.*)

1. GET READY TO READ ABOUT: Privacy

Exercise A (p. 16) (*Answers vary.*)

Exercise B (p. 16)
1. thinks   3. individual
2. personal   4. freedom

2. BUILDING READING SKILLS: Predicting

Practice Previewing and Predicting (p. 17)
I will learn about the American practice of friends calling each other before paying a visit. I will find out what the author thinks about this.

Use Your Reading Skills
Exercise A (p. 17)
1. Privacy
2. (*Answers vary.*)
3. (*Answers vary.*)

Exercise B (p. 17) (*Answers vary.*)

4. PROCESS WHAT YOU READ

Exercise A (p. 19)
1. d   2. f   3. a   4. e   5. c   6. b

Exercise B (p. 19)
1. c   2. b   3. c

Exercise C (p. 19) (*Answers vary.*)

5. WORK WITH THE VOCABULARY

Exercise A (p. 20)
a. believe   e. organization
b. act   f. information
d. protect

Exercise B (p. 20)
1. a. believe   b. belief
2. a. act   b. actions
3. a. protection   b. protect
4. a. inform   b. information
5. a. expression   b. express
6. a. organize   b. organization

Exercise C (p. 20)
1. c   2. d   3. e   4. b   5. a

6. GET READY TO READ ABOUT: Good Neighbors (p. 21) (*Answers vary.*)

Use Your Reading Skills
Exercise A (p. 21)
1. c   2. c   3. b   4. a

Exercise B (p. 21) (*Answers vary.*)

Exercise C (p. 21) (*Answers vary.*)

8. PROCESS WHAT YOU READ

Exercise A (p. 23)

7, 6, 2, 4, 3, 5, 1

Exercise B (p. 23)

1. because they spend too much time trying to get over, around or through the tall fence; a shorter fence will keep their son safe, and it will also let them visit easily with their neighbors (lines 22–34); Carol's parents disagree because it takes away from their privacy (lines 54–55)
2. she has pleasant talks, shares cups of coffee, and has supper in the backyard with her neighbors (lines 42–48)

9. WORK WITH THE VOCABULARY (p. 23)

more desirable	happier
more private	easier
more difficult	friendlier
shorter	better

11. GET READY TO READ AND SHARE

Exercise A (p. 24) (Answers vary.)

Exercise B (p. 24) (Answers vary.)

Exercise C (p. 24)

1. privacy on the Internet/online
2. communities on the Internet

Exercise D (p. 24) (Answers vary.)

13. SHARE WHAT YOU LEARNED (p. 27)

Focus Questions for Text A

1. because people can get their personal information from the Internet
2. they put "cookies" on the user's computer that tell the company what the user is buying or looking at on the Internet
3. by telling the computer not to accept cookies; by using false names; or by buying special computer programs that keep the user's identity a secret
4. that the Internet is similar to a public street—information they put in their computers can become public information

Focus Questions for Text B

1. everyone knew everyone else in a small town in the U.S.; community was an important part of life
2. because they watch TV, shop at big national chains, commute long distances to work or school,

and spend all their time working at the computer
3. a group of Internet users who send messages to each other about their lives; they have similar interests, ideas, or questions
4. they may focus on a health issue, try to make political changes, or offer help when a community member needs it

14. SHARE WHAT YOU THINK

(Answers vary.)

15. REFLECT ON WHAT YOU READ IN THIS UNIT

(Answers vary.)

Unit 3 Families that Work

WHAT DO YOU KNOW ABOUT TWO-INCOME FAMILIES?

Exercise A (p. 29) (Answers vary.)

Exercise B (p. 29)

1. d 2. c 3. e 4. a 5. b

1. GET READY TO READ ABOUT: Gender Roles

Exercise A (p. 30) (Answers vary.)

Exercise B (p. 30)

1. c 2. f 3. a 4. e 5. b 6. d

2. BUILDING READING SKILLS: More Previewing Strategies

Practice Previewing and Predicting

Exercise B (p. 31)

a, b, d

Exercise C (p. 31) (Answers vary.)

Use Your Reading Skills

Exercise A (p. 31)

a, c

Exercise B (p. 31)

a) lines 3–4, c) lines 15–16

4. PROCESS WHAT YOU READ

Exercise A (p. 33)

1. ~~men~~	women
2. ~~less~~	more
3. ~~gender~~	age
4. ~~after~~	before
5. ~~easier~~	more difficult/harder
6. ~~want~~	don't want

Exercise B (p. 33) (Answers vary.)

Exercise C (p. 33) (Answers vary.)

5. WORK WITH THE VOCABULARY (p. 33)

1. age	4. fine
2. agreement	5. hobby
3. single	

6. GET READY TO READ ABOUT: Stay-At-Home-Dads (p. 34)

1. c 2. a 3. d 4. b

7. BUILDING READING SKILLS: Previewing Questions

Practice Previewing Comprehension Questions (p. 34)

b

Use Your Reading Skills (p. 34)

(See p. 36 Process What You Read, Exercise A)

9. PROCESS WHAT YOU READ

Exercise A (p. 36)

1. d 2. b 3. c 4. a 5. b 6. b

Exercise B (p. 36)

1. (Answers vary.)
2. Yes. The author says "Wertman's book is entertaining and educational…"

10. WORK WITH THE VOCABULARY (p. 37)

1. a 2. d 3. b 4. d 5. d 6. c

11. GET READY TO READ AND SHARE

Exercise A (p. 38) (Answers vary.)

Exercise B (p. 38) (Answers vary.)

Exercise C (p. 38)

1. family businesses
2. companies that hire family members

Exercise D (p. 38) (Answers vary.)

14. SHARE WHAT YOU LEARNED (p. 41)

Focus Questions for Text A

1. siblings fight over the business, the family doesn't have a good business plan, or the younger generation isn't interested in the business
2. a flower shop; the Gioa brothers run the business
3. because the Gioas work hard; their mother and other relatives work with them, and they are teaching their young nephew the business
4. because the child learns responsibility

Focus Questions for Text B

1. fights between couples, battles between siblings, and favoritism.
2. Southwest Airlines, DoubleTree Hotel, Quad/Graphics.
3. 1) if the mother/father is a great worker, the daughter/son will probably be a great worker, 2) family ties keep employees

honest, and 3) when family members work together they're less likely to leave the company.
4. when they are successful (like Quad/Graphics)

15. SHARE WHAT YOU THINK
(*Answers vary.*)

16. REFLECT ON WHAT YOU READ IN THIS UNIT
(*Answers vary.*)

Unit 4 Staying in Business

WHAT DO YOU KNOW ABOUT BUSINESS?
Exercise A (p. 43) (*Answers vary.*)
Exercise B (p. 43) (*Answers vary.*)

1. GET READY TO READ ABOUT: Business in the U.S.
Exercise A (p. 44)
1. F   2. T   3. F   4. T
5. F   6. F   7. T   8. F
Exercise B (p. 44)
1. a   2. b   3. b   4. a   5. a   6. b

2. BUILDING READING SKILLS: Scanning
Practice Your Scanning Skills
Exercise A (p. 45)
1. Melodylights
2. Domino Parroti
Exercise B (p. 45)
1. 12   2. 10
Exercise C (p. 45)
1. $2.95   2. 100%
Use Your Reading Skills
Exercise A (p. 45)
The History of Big Business in the U.S.
Exercise B (p. 45)
1. 25 million immigrants
2. 20 millionaires

4. PROCESS WHAT YOU READ
Exercise A (p. 47)
1. b   2. a   3. c   4. c
Exercise B (p. 47)
1. more products, more customers, and more money
2. 3,000 millionaires
3. 20 cents an hour
4. 60 hours a week

5. WORK WITH THE VOCABULARY (p. 47)
1. improve   4. profit
2. owner   5. conditions
3. sell   6. work

6. GET READY TO READ ABOUT: A Business
Exercise A (p. 48)
1. a   2. b   3. e   4. c   5. d
Exercise B (p. 48) (*Answers vary.*)
Use Your Reading Skills (p. 48)
Exercise A (p. 48)
1. b   2. a
Exercise B (p. 48)
1. 1918   2. 61%

8. PROCESS WHAT YOU READ
Exercise A (p. 50)
1. a   2. b   3. c   4. a   5. c   6. c
Exercise B (p. 50)
1. They're disposable.
2. Their product was more successful.
3. (*Answers vary.*)
4. (*Answers vary.*)

9. WORK WITH THE VOCABULARY
Exercise A (p. 51)
1. substitute for
2. came up with
3. business is business
4. sales soared'
5. have a nose for
6. nothing to sneeze at
Exercise B (p. 51)
1. disposable   4. prefer
2. removable   5. washable
3. changeable

10. GET READY TO READ AND SHARE
Exercise A (p. 52) (*Answers vary.*)
Exercise B (p. 52) (*Answers vary.*)
Exercise C (p. 52)
1. about how men and women think
2. about how men and women communicate
3. a researcher and consultant
Exercise D (p. 52) (*Answers vary.*)

13. SHARE WHAT YOU LEARNED (p. 55)
Focus Questions for Text A
1. 30 years ago, almost all business owners, company presidents, managers and supervisors were men
2. Blue thinking: people shouldn't share their weaknesses; powerful people always get respect; it's important to make friends with people in power; the team is more important than the individual
Pink thinking: when people talk about their weaknesses they

form a connection; when someone is wrong, it doesn't matter if he or she is the boss, it's important to say so; people shouldn't make friends just to help their careers; the team matters but the individual is important too
3. because half the people in any company may have a different thinking style from the other half

Focus Questions for Text B
1. because before 1970 men were in charge of most companies and blue is the typical style of communication for men
2. blues use short direct messages; they rarely talk about their personal lives at work; blues don't think everyone needs to agree.
3. pinks have a more informal style of conversation; they believe that most work conversations should begin with small talk about their personal lives; pinks will try to get everyone to agree
4. people should use their own communication style to restate the messages they hear

14. SHARE WHAT YOU THINK
(*Answers vary.*)

15. REFLECT ON WHAT YOU READ IN THIS UNIT
(*Answers vary.*)

Unit 5 Staying Healthy

WHAT DO YOU KNOW ABOUT STAYING HEALTHY?
Exercise A (p. 57) (*Answers vary.*)
Exercise B (p. 57) (*Answers vary.*)

1. GET READY TO READ ABOUT: Quackery
Exercise A (p. 58) (*Answers vary.*)
Exercise B (p. 58)
1. secret   4. painless
2. ingredients   5. effective
3. miracle
Exercise C (p. 58) (*Answers vary.*)

2. BUILDING READING SKILLS: Finding Clues in Context
Practice Finding Clues From Context (p. 59)
1. a headache
2. reasons for
3. poor air quality, lights, too much noise
4. a person's feelings or emotions

Use Your Reading Skills

Exercise A (p. 59)

1. Medical quackery or fake doctors
2. *(Answers vary.)*

Exercise B (p. 59)

1. phony doctor
2. fast and easy cure
3. people who live in cities
4. a powerful drug
5. a radioactive element
6. against the law

4. PROCESS WHAT YOU READ

Exercise A (p. 61)

1. quacks; they "cured"people who secretly worked for them to convince other people to buy a medicine
2. diseases spread quickly in the cities, so people were scared so they bought anything they though would protect or cure them
3. the U.S. government made it illegal to sell false medicine or lie about its ingredients
4. no, people continue to buy things that promise them they will feel or look better

Exercise B (p. 61)

(Answers vary.)

5. WORK WITH THE VOCABULARY (p. 61)

1. c   2. d   3. b   4. e   5. f   6. a

6. GET READY TO READ ABOUT: Stress

Exercise A (p. 62) *(Answers vary.)*

Exercise B (p. 62) *(Answers vary.)*

Use Your Reading Skills

Exercise A (p. 62)

1, 4, 5

Exercise B (p. 62)

1. serious illness, death, earthquakes, or wars
2. when people can't control it
3. to stay alive
4. to run away

8. PROCESS WHAT YOU READ

Exercise A (p. 64)

1. when it is unmanageable.
2. it helps people to survive; when you are in danger, changes in your body prepare you to fight or run away
3. the heart rate, blood pressure, blood sugar, and the need for oxygen increase
4. deep breathing and muscle relaxation
5. cutting down on sugar and caffeine

6. because you can use relaxation techniques or exercises before you feel "stressed out"

Exercise B (p. 64)

Paragraph 1: d	Paragraph 4: b
Paragraph 2: e	Paragraph 5: c
Paragraph 3: a	

Exercise C (p. 64) *(Answers vary.)*

Exercise D (p. 64) *(Answers vary.)*

9. WORK WITH THE VOCABULARY

Exercise A (p. 65)

1. c   2. d   3. f   4. e   5. a   6. b

Exercise B (p. 65)

1. unmanageable   4. unattractive
2. unsafe   5. unimportant
3. unsuccessful

Exercise C (p. 65)

unbelievable	unhealthy
uninterested	unwell
unmanageable	unhappy

10. GET READY TO READ AND SHARE

Exercise A (p. 66) *(Answers vary.)*

Exercise B (p. 66) *(Answers vary.)*

Exercise C (p. 66)

1. The topic of Text A is support groups. The topic of Text B is the connection between laughter and good health.
2. *(Answers vary.)*

Exercise D (p. 66) *(Answers vary.)*

14. SHARE WHAT YOU LEARNED (p. 69)

Focus Questions for Text A

1. a group of people with similar problems who meet to help each other
2. to get understanding, information, and advice
3. Alcoholics Anonymous; it started when two men met and talked about their experiences with alcohol
4. support groups for medical conditions and for the families of people who are ill

Focus Questions for Text B

1. relieve pain and reduce stress
2. it creates new cells and helps create antibodies that fight off disease
3. because they want to get well and stay well
4. they learn exercises that will help them laugh.

14. SHARE WHAT YOU THINK

(Answers vary.)

15. REFLECT ON WHAT YOU READ IN THIS UNIT

(Answers vary.)

Unit 6   One of a Kind

DO YOU THINK INDIVIDUALITY IS IMPORTANT?

Exercise A (p. 71) *(Answers vary.)*

Exercise B (p. 71) *(Answers vary.)*

1. GET READY TO READ ABOUT: Individuality

Exercise A (p. 72)

1. the qualities that make one person different from another
2. separate person
3. make general statements that are untrue.
4. negative opinion of a group of people based on their race, religion, or gender.
5. forcing [them] to work without pay and selling [them] as property
6. couldn't get the same jobs as males
7. right to vote, say what they think, and get fair and equal treatment by the government
8. think of older people as problems rather than valuable and productive members of society.
9. obey
10. groups represent different races, nations, tribes and regions

Exercise B (p. 72) *(Answers vary.)*

2. BUILDING READING SKILLS: Inferring

Practice Inferring (p. 73)

1. no; he was alive in the 1850's
2. because Washington is the capital of the United States
3. no
4. slaves didn't go to school
5. she wanted people to know that slavery was wrong
6. yes (she ran away and she spoke out)

Use Your Reading Skills

Exercise A (p. 73)

1. the importance of an individual
2. *(Answers vary.)*

Exercise B (p. 73) *(Answers vary.)*

4. PROCESS WHAT YOU READ

Exercise A (p. 75)

1. as individuals first, and then as members of various groups
2. they make choices and give their opinions almost from the time they begin to talk

3. Peter Pitchlynn was an advocate for Native American rights; Sojourner Truth spoke out against slavery; Elizabeth Cady Stanton was an advocate for women's right to vote; Cesar Chavez was an advocate for farm workers' rights
4. racism, ageism, and sexism are enemies of individuality; teachers, civil rights workers, and lawyers fight against them.

Exercise B (p. 75)

Paragraph 1: c   Paragraph 4: b
Paragraph 2: e   Paragraph 5: d
Paragraph 3: a

Exercise C (p. 75)

(Answers vary. Some examples are:)
1. family groups, religious groups, political groups, etc.
2. they choose what clothes to wear, what foods to eat, which toys to play with, etc.
3. you don't need money or power to succeed
4. teachers can fight discrimination in the classroom and reach many young people; lawyers can help people fight in the courts; it's the job of a civil rights worker to fight discrimination

5. WORK WITH THE VOCABULARY

Exercise A (p. 76)

1. a   2. b   3. a   4. a   5. b   6. a

Exercise B (p. 76)

1. e   2. d   3. c   4. a
5. f   6. h   7. b   8. g

6. GET READY TO READ ABOUT: A Unique Man

Exercise A (p. 77) *(Answers vary.)*
Exercise B (p. 77) *(Answers vary.)*

Use Your Reading Skills (p. 77)
1. b   2. b   3. a   4. c

8. PROCESS WHAT YOU READ (p. 79)

1. b   2. b   3. a   4. b   5. a

9. WORK WITH THE VOCABULARY (p. 79)

1. ordinary   3. boring
2. similar   4. typical

10. GET READY TO READ AND SHARE

Exercise A (p. 80) *(Answers vary.)*
Exercise B (p. 80) *(Answers vary.)*

Exercise C (p. 80)
1. Text A is about Cora Wilson Stewart. Text B is about Walt Whitman.
2. Cora Stewart started the Moonlight Schools for adults. Walt Whitman was a famous American poet.

Exercise D (p. 80) *(Answers vary.)*

13. SHARE WHAT YOU LEARNED (p. 83)

Focus Questions for Text A
1. in 1875 in Kentucky
2. that many of the parents of the children in her schools could not read or write; she wanted to help these people, so she asked teachers to volunteer to teach reading and writing to adults.
3. she started the first literacy classes for adults and developed special materials to help adults learn to read and write

Focus Questions for Text B
1. on May 31, 1819 on Long Island in New York
2. an office boy, a printer a teacher, a newspaper journalist, a short story writer, a newspaper editor, and a house builder; these jobs taught him about different types of Americans
3. through this poetry he celebrated the American cities, farmlands, people and everyday events.

14. SHARE WHAT YOU THINK *(Answers vary.)*

15. REFLECT ON WHAT YOU READ IN THIS UNIT *(Answers vary.)*

Unit 7 Learning to Learn

WHAT ARE YOUR IDEAS ABOUT EDUCATION?

Exercise A (p. 85) *(Answers vary.)*
Exercise B (p. 85) *(Answers vary.)*

1. GET READY TO READ ABOUT: Education

Exercise A (p. 86) *(Answers vary.)*
Exercise B (p. 86)
1. a   2. c   3. b   4. a   5. a

2. BUILDING READING SKILLS: Finding the Main Idea

Practice Finding the Main Idea and Supporting Ideas (p. 87)
1. b   2. b

Use Your Reading Skills (p. 87)
Exercise A (p. 87)
1. Diversity in Colleges and Universities
2. *(Answers vary.)*
Exercise B (p. 87) *(Answers vary.)*

4. PROCESS WHAT YOU READ

Exercise A (p. 89)
1. it includes students from different ethnicities and income levels
2. only wealthy white males
3. Radcliffe and Howard.
4. to pay tuition and living costs for any World War II veteran who wanted to go to college
5. the number doubled between
6. because education equals opportunity.

Exercise B (p. 89)
1. ~~similar~~   diverse
2. ~~women~~   men
3. ~~high school~~   college
4. ~~quickly~~   slowly
5. ~~decreasing~~   increasing
6. ~~diversity~~   opportunity

Exercise C (p. 89)
(Answers vary.)

5. WORK WITH THE VOCABULARY (p. 90)

Exercise A (p. 90)
a. diverse
b. wealthy
c. ethnic
d. equal
e. national

Exercise B (p. 90)
1. wealthy   4. diversity
2. diverse   5. wealth
3. ethnic

Exercise C (p. 90)
1. diverse
2. diversity
3. national, wealthy
4. wealth
5. equality
6. ethnicity
7. nation
8. equality, ethnicity

6. GET READY TO READ ABOUT: College Life

Exercise A (p. 91)
(Answers vary.)
Exercise B (p. 91)
1. b   2. c   3. a   4. c

Use Your Reading Skills (p. 91)
2 and 4 are not in the article.

8. PROCESS WHAT YOU READ
(p. 93)

1. c   2. b   3. b   4. a   5. b

9. WORK WITH THE VOCABULARY (p. 93)

1. stories
2. socialize
3. nonacademic activities
4. a necessary and important part

10. GET READY TO READ AND SHARE

Exercise A (p. 94) *(Answers vary.)*
Exercise B (p. 94) *(Answers vary.)*
Exercise C (p. 94)

1. learning styles.
2. multiple intelligences.

Exercise D (p. 94) *(Answers vary.)*

13. SHARE WHAT YOU LEARNED (p. 97)

Focus Questions for Text A
1. people learn in different ways—there are visual, auditory, and tactile learners; it's important to know how you learn best in order to improve your study skills.
2. by studying different student behaviors
3. Visual learners prefer to learn by seeing new information; auditory learners prefer to hear new information; tactile learners prefer to learn by touching

Focus Questions for Text B
1. the traditional views of intelligence are changing—the theory of Multiple Intelligences shows different ways people are intelligent; researchers now know that there is more than one kind of intelligence; this information is changing the American classroom
2. What are the things people do in the world? What abilities do you need to do those things?
3. (see chart on p. 96 for intelligences)

14. SHARE WHAT YOU THINK
(Answers vary.)

15. REFLECT ON WHAT YOU READ IN THIS UNIT
(Answers vary.)

Unit 8 Play Time

HOW DO YOU FEEL ABOUT TIME?
Exercise A (p. 99) *(Answers vary.)*
Exercise B (p. 99) *(Answers vary.)*

1. GET READY TO READ ABOUT: Vacations

Exercise A (p. 100)
(Answers vary.)
Exercise B (p. 100)
1. b   2. b   3. a   4. b   5. a   6. b
Exercise C (p. 100)
(Answers vary.)

2. BUILDING READING SKILLS: Summarizing

Practice Finding the Main Idea and Supporting Ideas
Exercise A (p. 101) *(Answers vary.)*
Exercise B (p. 101) *(Answers vary.)*

Use Your Reading Skills (p. 101)
(See answers for Exercise A, p. 103)

4. PROCESS WHAT YOU READ

Exercise A (p. 103)
1. Puritan values do not support the idea of "getting away from it all"
2. wealthy people from the cities; they went to their country homes in the summer
3. people did not say they were going on vacations—they said they were "going away for their health"
4. in the middle of the 20th century; they went camping in a national park or stayed in an inexpensive motel
5. some people believe that they have to be productive on their vacations
6. Americans like to add work to their play

Exercise B (p. 103) *(Answers vary.)*
Exercise C (p. 103)

Paragraph 2: a   Paragraph 4: c
Paragraph 3. b   Paragraph 5: b

5. WORK WITH THE VOCABULARY (P. 104)

Exercise A (p. 104)
1. e   2. d   3. b   4. c   5. a
Exercise B (p. 104)
1. c   2. e   3. b   4. f   5. a   6. d

6. GET READY TO READ ABOUT: Space Vacations

Exercise A (p. 105)
(Answers vary.)
Exercise B (p. 105)
(Answers vary.)

Use Your Reading Skills (p. 105)
(See answers for Exercise A, p. 107)

8. PROCESS WHAT YOU READ
(p. 107)

Exercise A (p. 107)
1. F   2. T   3. T   4. T   5. T   6. F
Exercise B (p. 107)

~~relaxing~~	relaxing
~~weekly~~	daily
~~increase~~	reduce
~~reduce~~	increase
~~satellite repair~~	recreation
~~20th~~	21st
~~2020~~	2010

9. WORK WITH THE VOCABULARY (p. 107)

1. e   2. g   3. h   4. f
5. c   6. b   7. d   8. a

10. GET READY TO READ AND SHARE

Exercise A (p. 108) *(Answers vary.)*
Exercise B (p. 108) *(Answers vary.)*
Exercise C (p. 108)

1. volunteer vacations
2. the free time

Exercise D (p. 108) *(Answers vary.)*

14. SHARE WHAT YOU LEARNED (p. 111)

Focus Questions for Text A
1. working to help others without getting paid; over one-third of Americans volunteer
2. a vacation dedicated to helping preserve and protect America's environment, culture, or history, e.g., working in national parks and whale counting
3. because they like to add work to play and feel productive

Focus Questions for Text B
1. that technology would create more free time
2. when people don't have enough time; free time decreased almost 40% over the past 20 years
3. they are: choosing to have fewer possessions and work less, making time for family and friends, turning off their cell phones and taking time for leisure activities

14. SHARE WHAT YOU THINK
(Answers vary.)

15. REFLECT ON WHAT YOU READ IN THIS UNIT
(Answers vary.)

Teacher's Notes

The Thinking Behind *Read and Reflect*

Read and Reflect follows current second-language reading pedagogy by ensuring that students:

- activate their background knowledge before and while they read.
- learn and apply effective reading strategies.
- read silently and with a purpose.
- interact with the material while they read.
- expand their active and passive vocabulary.
- check their comprehension of a text.
- analyze, synthesize, and/or evaluate the author's ideas.

The texts in *Read and Reflect* are adapted from or modeled after authentic texts, such as newspaper and magazine articles, web pages, and encyclopedia articles. This is done to give beginning-level students as real a reading experience as possible. The flow and voice of the original materials were retained in the adapted texts, while the vocabulary and grammar were adjusted to match the students' level.

In *Read and Reflect*, students are encouraged to read silently because the reading of a text is intended to be a silent interaction between the reader and the text (except in the case of poetry or reading to an audience). Although reading an individual word or single sentence aloud can help students' comprehension, reading an entire text aloud does not increase students' reading proficiency and is not emphasized in this book.

The variety of vocabulary exercises in *Read and Reflect*, as well as the wealth of contextualized vocabulary in the texts, assist students in the development of active and passive vocabulary. Getting meaning from context is a key reading strategy. Right from the beginning, students are encouraged to determine the meaning of new words from context rather than relying on their dictionaries. While students are given the opportunity to work with a dictionary in some pre-reading activities, reliance on the dictionary *while* reading often prevents the experience from being fluent and effective. In addition, academic words (e.g., create, identify, respond, summarize, etc.) are introduced in order to help students prepare for academic reading in their English and content-based classes.

Book 1 of *Read and Reflect* lays a foundation for the development of critical literacy by having students examine the source of a text in relationship to the ideas and opinions expressed within the text. It also provides opportunities for students to consider and clarify their own opinions, attitudes and values in relation to the text.

Teaching from *Read and Reflect*

Read and Reflect provides instructional flexibility, allowing you to tailor the activities to your classroom setting and your students' needs. One need universal to all students is to understand the purpose of their learning. The "To the Student" page (p. vi) introduces the purpose of this series and provides suggestions to help students read better. You can also reinforce this concept in class and emphasize the goals of each unit before you teach it, and point out how students have met those goals at the end of the unit.

A Tour of the Unit

The unit tour below outlines the purpose of each type of activity and provides teaching suggestions.

OPENING PAGE

The goals on the opening page identify the unit's cultural theme and reading strategies. The cartoon or illustration on the page prompts students to think about and discuss what they already know about the theme of the unit.

Teaching Suggestions
- The unit title expresses the theme of the unit, and in several instances the title is an idiomatic expression as well. In order to model previewing, elicit the meaning of the titles from the class.

- Go over the appropriate language and non-verbal behavior for stating opinions and agreeing or disagreeing with others, before having students engage in the discussion activities on this page.

- To ensure greater participation in discussions in the beginning level classroom, give students time to think or write about their responses to discussion questions before they speak. This usually leads to a greater number of students being able to participate in the discussion. Another way to ensure participation is to have one student respond to a question and have five or six other students create a chain of responses based on what the first student said. For example, if Jose says "I think everyone who succeeds in school will succeed at work. What do you think, Pat?" Pat can say, " I agree with you. What do you think, Tanya?" Tanya may say, "I disagree. I think you can succeed at work without school. What do you think, Mario?" etc.

GET READY TO READ

Before reading the first and second texts of the unit, students complete pre-reading activities that activate their prior knowledge about the reading topics and expose them to key vocabulary.

Teaching Suggestions

- In the exercises, students are often asked to guess meanings of vocabulary they will encounter in the text. Ask students to check their guesses once they have had an opportunity to read the material. Then give them a chance to share with a partner or with the class whether they guessed correctly.

- Another type of vocabulary activity in this section has students work in pairs or teams to discuss the meanings of words they know from a list of key vocabulary. Then they look up the words they don't know in a dictionary. Encourage students to ask other teams or pairs to define words they don't know before looking them up.

BUILDING READING SKILLS

This page introduces important reading skills, such as previewing or scanning, and explains the strategies students can use to implement these skills. For example, looking for specific signals,

such as numbers to find dates, times, or prices in a text, is a strategy for scanning. After students practice the strategies, they apply the new reading strategies (as well as strategies from previous units) in the Use Your Reading Skills exercises. All reading skills and strategies are recycled throughout the book in order to give students as many opportunities as possible to learn and use the skills.

Teaching Suggestions

- Provide an example of the reading skill and strategies in the unit, before having students read about them. For example, for previewing, show students a large newspaper headline or picture and have them tell you what the newspaper article is about. For scanning, put an advertisement on the overhead projector or board and have students tell you the cost of the advertised item. Name the strategy students are employing and explain the rationale for using it. Elicit situations in which students have used the same strategy.

- Periodically review the strategies the students have learned. Ask students to monitor their use of these strategies in their reading outside of class and encourage students to identify the ways these strategies help their reading comprehension.

READ

The four theme-related texts in each unit help students deepen their understanding of the theme, read with greater comprehension, and internalize recycled vocabulary. The first text is typically an academic text such as an encyclopedia or textbook article. The second text is usually lighter in tone and often has a more conversational style; for example, an editorial or personal essay. The third and fourth texts are part of the Read and Share activity (see next page) but may also be taught as independent texts.

Important vocabulary in the texts is either introduced in the pre-reading activities or presented in context. Difficult content words that are key to students' understanding, but are not high frequency words, are glossed. Words that are not important to a general understanding of a text are left undefined and students are expected to skip over them.

Teaching Suggestions

- To help students get the most meaning from their reading, show them how to use the glossaries on the page, and then ask them to read the text once silently. Tell them to read without looking up unknown words.

- Set a time limit for students to read the text and answer the questions. A time limit requires students to finish at the same time so that they can begin their pair or group work simultaneously.

- Once students have read the text, have them work on the Process What You Read questions. Encourage them to answer all the questions first and then go back to check their answers against the text. They can check in pairs or small groups. Explain that this procedure will help them evaluate how much of the text they understood.

- Once the processing questions have been answered and checked, you can read the text aloud to the class while they follow along silently. As you read, model some "think aloud" techniques, such as asking yourself the following types of questions aloud, *I wonder if that's true?* or *What is the author telling me?* This will help students understand the thinking processes used by effective readers.

- If time permits, allow students to read the text a third time, circling five words they want to add to their active vocabulary. Give students time to record these words and their definitions in a separate section of their notebooks.

PROCESS WHAT YOU READ

After reading the first and second text in each unit, students do exercises to check their comprehension and use their higher-level thinking skills to analyze or evaluate the information they read. The first time an exercise type is introduced in the book, a sample answer is given.

Teaching Suggestions

- For the first exercise of this section, encourage students to do the exercise individually, and then to look back at the text to check their answers with a partner or teammates.

- For sentence-level writing practice, have students write answers to questions in their notebooks. They can correct their answers by first looking back at the text and then checking the Answer Key. Students can also check their answers with a partner, which will create discussion opportunities.

- In this section, there is usually a second exercise, which is intended to help students think critically about the text. To ensure that every student has a chance to think about the topic, tell students to first answer the questions individually, and then discuss their answers with a partner, a small group, or the whole class.

- In order to help develop students' critical literacy, each text has brief introductory material identifying its source or the author's background. To help students develop critical literacy, ask them questions such as: *Why does the author ask so many questions in the last paragraph?* (Unit 2, Text 2) or *Do encyclopedia articles usually have facts or opinions?* (Unit 4, Text 1).

WORK WITH THE VOCABULARY

After reading the first and second text in each unit, students increase their active vocabulary through a variety of exercises. These include working with definitions, synonyms, word families, prefixes, and context clues.

Teaching Suggestions

- Encourage students to keep a journal of vocabulary words including those presented in this section, the glossed words, and other words from the text. Then have students note each time they encounter these words in their reading outside of class.

- Recycle the words students learn in each unit in other class activities. This will increase the likelihood of new words becoming part of your students' active vocabulary.

READ AND SHARE

These four pages comprise a highly effective and communicative technique for developing reading proficiency. The Read and Share technique follows these steps:

Get Ready to Read and Share

1. Students complete general pre-reading and vocabulary activities.

2. They preview two complimentary texts in order to select one to read.

3. Along with the information gleaned in their preview, the students use guiding questions and open-ended statements to learn more about the text they selected.

Read A/Read B

4. Students choose a topic to read and read with the purpose of learning new information and then sharing it with a partner.

Share What You Learned

5. When the class finishes reading, each student finds a partner who has read the same text and they work in pairs to answer the focus questions relating to their text.

6. Students then work with another pair that has read the complimentary text. The pairs take turns sharing what they have read, using the focus questions to guide their presentation.

Share What You Think

7. In small groups or as a whole class, students use what they have learned from the texts as well as their background knowledge and personal experience to respond to follow-up questions.

Teaching Suggestions

- Each time students do a Read and Share activity, remind them of the purpose for the activity. Tell students that during the Read and Share they will choose one of two texts and work with a partner to answer questions about the text. Once they understand the most important ideas in their text, they will share these ideas with a pair of students who read the other text.

- This activity works best if students choose their own text; however, this can be tricky if most students prefer one text over another (20 students pick A, 3 pick B). If fewer than a third of the students pick one of the texts, ask for volunteers to read the less popular text, assuring students that they can read their first choice the next time. If you prefer not to leave the selection to chance, you can assign A/B roles to students.

- To give students an additional reading opportunity, you can assign the complimentary text as an in-class activity or as homework.

- From time to time you may want to have all students read the A and B texts sequentially instead of as a Read and Share activity. In this case, have students read one text and answer the corresponding focus questions. It may be helpful to put the focus questions for the selected text on the board or overhead. Then repeat the process for the other text.

REFLECT ON WHAT YOU READ IN THIS UNIT

This page provides three types of activities that help students synthesize the ideas within the unit: interviewing, charting and writing. In the interview activity, students work in pairs or small groups to ask and answer questions that relate their personal experiences to the cultural focus of the unit. For the charting activity, students create charts and diagrams that show their responses to questions about an aspect of the unit's cultural focus. The writing activity begins with a pre-writing discussion and uses questions to help students construct a paragraph that reflects the unit theme.

Teaching Suggestions

- Different activity types on this page will appeal to different students. You may find that students are more successful if they select one of the three activities to complete.

- The writing activity is guided, so it can be assigned as homework; however, the pre-writing activity allows for discussion about the writing topic and is most effective if done in class.